D0421974

ZOO MAN

ZOO MAN

INSIDE THE ZOO REVOLUTION

TERRY L. MAPLE, PH.D.,
AND ERIKA F. ARCHIBALD

LONGSTREET PRESS
Atlanta, Georgia

To the memory of
Professor Dr. Heini Hediger,
and to the zoo men and women everywhere
who are still inspired by his ideas

Published by
LONGSTREET PRESS, INC.
A subsidiary of Cox Newspapers,
A division of Cox Enterprises, Inc.
2140 Newmarket Parkway
Suite 118
Marietta, GA 30067

Printed in the United States of America
1st printing 1993
Library of Congress Catalog Card Number: 91-61926
ISBN 1-56352-076-1

This book was printed by R. R. Donnelley & Sons, Harrisonburg, Virginia.

Book design and typesetting by Jill Dible.

Frontispiece: *Terry L. Maple and Starlet the elephant. Starlet was named in a public contest and now lives with Victoria and Zambezi in the zoo's Mzima Springs Exhibit.*

CONTENTS

PREFACE

A book is finally written in a quiet place with pen in hand or word processor at arm's length, but it is surely formulated in a myriad of different ways. This book took shape in peaceful walks among the hardwoods, in meditative sessions among the great apes, through sleepless nights of genuine conflict, confined within big-bodied aircraft in the path of another adventure, in the give and take of a furious debate, and in my basement at Mariposa, my tranquil, wooded residence on the eastern outskirts of Atlanta.

I'm a lucky guy. I've been a teacher for twenty-four years. As a college professor, I have been encouraged to think, write, lecture, and counsel. I prepared ten years for the professional life, and I continue to enjoy the company of my colleagues and students. To be sure, there is pressure in the academy. Publish or perish is the law of the blackboard jungle. Productivity and quality are required for advancement, but professors control their own destiny. Paychecks may be powerful motivators, but autonomy is what most folks desire in the workplace. My old friend Larry James, an industrial-organizational psychologist by trade, once advised me that no one enjoys more autonomy than a successful college professor.

I never aspired to be a zoo director, but it has been the highlight of my professional life. There is an unruly side of me that requires action beyond the so-called ivory tower. The zoo world is wild, chaotic, and fun. It can also be painful and volatile. I live in two worlds now, one more predictable and orderly, the other a roller coaster of emotional highs and lows—higher than I have ever known and lower than I could have imagined. Surprisingly, the zoo and the university are a good and natural fit. I am a professor in the zoo, and I will always be a teaching zoo director.

Zoo Man is about building a zoo in the latter part of the

twentieth century. In the 1970s and early 1980s the Atlanta Zoo was a disaster, and this book chronicles its turnaround success beginning in 1984, when a new zoo team transformed it into Zoo Atlanta. But Atlanta's fascinating zoo story is not isolated; it is part of an international zoo revolution. So *Zoo Man* is also my guided tour through the exciting changes zoos are making worldwide to provide refuges for our endangered wildlife. I have told Atlanta's story with revolutionary zeal. Thankfully, zoos are in the throes of gargantuan change, and these are exciting times to be a zoo man. I have written this book for everyday zoo visitors, people who want to know more about what is going on behind the scenes. I also had in mind future zoo board members, usually spirited community leaders who are experts in their field but fairly uninformed about the zoo profession. *Zoo Man* is the story of one person's experience in the zoo world, but it is intended as a primer about zoos today and tomorrow.

On the road to writing this book I've had a lot of help. Carolyn Boyd Hatcher invited me to be a zoo director. Carolyn's early confidence in me sustained my effort during the challenging first, dark days of my assignment. Even today, I continue to benefit from her sage counsel. My zoo life began in northern California, nurtured by Gary Mitchell, my mentor at the University of California at Davis, and by Bill Meeker, then director of the nearby Sacramento Zoo. Once Bill permitted me access through the back gate, I was hooked on the zoo. In the late 1970s, I was influenced by a young zoo director, Ron Forman, who was skillfully transforming the Audubon Zoo in New Orleans. While on leave from Georgia Tech, I worked for Ron as deputy director and general curator. My contributions to the zoo were quite modest, but it was a wonderful opportunity to learn from one of the world's great zoo directors.

I am both a zoo director and a college professor because Ed Loveland and Andy Smith, the past and present directors of Georgia Tech's School of Psychology, encouraged me to merge the two disciplines. The zoo continues to be a laboratory where I can advance my ideas about the experience of captivity, organizational behavior, learning, management, and habitat design. Psychology certainly is compatible with zoo management.

Science looms large at Zoo Atlanta, but the business side is equally emphasized. My training continues with help from the brilliant business men and women who have served on the boards of Zoo Atlanta and the Friends of Zoo Atlanta. I thank them all for their support and guidance during the past nine years.

I owe many intellectual debts of gratitude. My efforts in zoodom continue to be inspired by the ideas of Heini Hediger. I thank Bob Sommer for first advising me to read Hediger's *Wild Animals in Captivity*. Hediger's publications and his personal encouragement are among my most powerful sources of motivation. Two noted zoo directors have counseled me over the years: Clayton Freiheit and Gary Clarke. Bob Wagner has also taken a personal interest in my career, and I appreciate the many times he took me aside to pass on a bit of wisdom. All young zoo directors should have such sagacious advisers.

Among my scientific peers—and good friends, too—Ben Beck, Joe Erwin, Don Lindburg, Hal Markowitz, and Christian Schmidt have helped me to improve my work. Designers Jon Coe and Gary Lee have had an enormous effect on the path of my career. The programming of Zoo Atlanta's exhibitry has been a very special experience because of the quality and depth of their ideas. In the zoo, my most valued collaborators have been Rita McManamon and Dietrich Schaaf. I can't imagine a Zoo Atlanta without them. Of course, my debt must be extended to all my staff, past and present, who have labored long and hard to create a world-class zoo in Atlanta.

My co-author in this endeavor, Erika Archibald, breathed life into this book when it was down-for-the-count. Erika knows the zoo well, having spent four years at the helm of our public information division, but her greatest skill is in managing a project. She oversaw this book to its completion and restructured its contents. Her lucid writing style dramatically improved the first author's original draft. This book is a record of my experiences in the zoo field. It is comprehensible only because Erika made it so.

Erika expresses her gratitude to her mother, who surrounded her with books and animals and a love for nature. She also acknowledges the love and support of her husband, Robin Sherman, and her animals William and Ethel. We both thank Veneita Mullins, who typed the original manuscript; Joe Sebo for photographic assistance; and Suzanne Comer Bell, whose sharp pencil defined its final form. My administrative assistant, Holly Harris, carefully reviewed the final draft and provided many helpful suggestions. Thanks also to Chuck Perry, whose patience and encouragement made this book possible.

Finally, I am grateful to my immediate family: Addie, Molly, Emily, Sally, and Jean. I'm grumpy when I write, and having labored at this task for more than a year, I apologize for gnashing my teeth and otherwise behaving like a baboon toward the end. Books emerge from my inner self in just this way. I wish it could be otherwise, but emerge it has, and I am much happier for the outcome.

To our readers, we hope you will treat this book like a zoo visit. You'll find many opportunities to learn herein, but it should be fun to read! For more information, and more fun, visit the zoo again and again. The zoo, after all, is the better teacher.

Terry L. Maple
Atlanta, Georgia
Spring 1993

ZOO MAN

THE ASCENDING PHOENIX

ZOO ATLANTA'S STORY

Atlanta has given neither money nor thought to its disintegrating zoo. How a community treats animals says something about the human beings who run it. Unless Atlanta wants to commit itself to a professionally operated zoological park, would it not be better to forget about having one at all?

New York Times, *June 1984*

One cold day in February 1984 I boarded a flight with a group of Atlanta Zoo supporters, folks who, like me, were interested in wildlife and conservation. We were all eager to begin our trip to Kenya, to spend two glorious weeks observing the magnificent animals of East Africa. As a professor of psychology at Georgia Tech and an animal behaviorist, I had agreed to lead a tour for the Atlanta Zoological Society and was looking forward to a great adventure. The flight took off and the group was in an upbeat mood, chattering among themselves. Then something terrible happened. One of the group members opened up the *Atlanta Journal and Constitution* and revealed a shocking story on the front page. The Atlanta Zoo had just been named one of the ten worst zoos in America. Worse yet, the list, compiled by the Humane Society of the United States, had been published for a national audience, in *Parade* magazine. Our zoo was being labeled a disaster, and they were telling all of America the whole story.

My traveling companions were suddenly silenced. As

long-time supporters and volunteers for the zoo, they were crestfallen. A few broke down and cried. How could this have happened? Was it really that bad?

In fact, I knew that it was. So did other insiders. Now, after the initial shock, I began to rejoice silently. Perhaps, I reasoned, something could finally be done. I was reminded of "The Emperor's New Clothes": The Atlanta Zoo was standing buck naked, exposed for all the world to see. Surely the city, our community, would realize that drastic changes were needed, that the zoo was crying out for help. Maybe, I thought, daring to dream a little, this could even be part of a revolution of sorts, where all kinds of zoo problems could be solved. Maybe others would see and be inspired to make better zoos elsewhere, too—for the sake of animals in tiny, unnatural exhibits and for the sake of people, who might not even know they were seeing some of the last representatives of dying breeds. Such were the musings on that long flight to meet the good earth's most magnificent wild creatures.

The story of the Atlanta Zoo is long and complicated. Because our zoo was founded by accident and thus never planned, and our knowledge of animals and people had advanced beyond our dilapidated facilities, we were long overdue for a zoo revolution.

In the spring of 1889, G. W. Hall's Circus and Bingley's English Menagerie rolled into Atlanta by rail, on its way to a performance in the nearby town of Marietta. But all was not well with the finances of "Popcorn George" and his circus, and the train was halted in Atlanta. Popcorn George found himself in a local court in a wage dispute, and his assets were subsequently confiscated. In that obscure moment of history, lions, pumas, wildcats, camels, two monkeys, one jaguar, gazelles, hyenas, and other animals found themselves without a home and up for sale at auction. A prominent local businessman by the name of G. V. Gress purchased the whole collection and decided to donate it to the city for display in L. P. Grant Park. So, the city erected a 100' x 40' building to house the animals, and the display soon became known as the Grant Park Zoo. The little building, housing animals from East Africa and South America, would stand for seventy more years, for most of that time as the principal exhibition building.

In many ways, though, these meager facilities of the old Atlanta Zoo were not unlike those of many other zoos, especially those that started small. Even the great San Diego Zoo had very modest beginnings, and it, too, was originally composed of surplus animals from a menagerie, in this case from the 1916 Panama-California International Exposition. Their original collection was described as including a "half dozen moth-eaten monkeys, coyotes and bears."

There was a big difference however, between the founding of the zoos in San Diego and Atlanta. San Diego's zoo was founded by a visionary, Dr. Harry Wegeforth, who publicly proclaimed his dreams. He wanted the San Diego Zoo to be world-class and announced that he would provide "more zoo for the money than any other in the world." Such ambition was a remarkable phenomenon for San Diego in the early twentieth century. San Diego Zoo historian Neil Morgan remarked in his 1953 book: "How wildly impossible it seemed to the people of San Diego in 1916 that so small a city, in a remote corner of the nation, should aspire to a zoological garden vying in importance with those of the world's oldest and largest cities."

But Dr. Wegeforth's aim was true. After just one year of operation, the San Diego Zoo was labeled by a press association as "the finest collection of animals on the West Coast." It was vision that made all the difference in San Diego.

The founding moments of a few other zoos were framed by

a larger vision. For example, the National Zoo in Washington, D.C., founded in 1889, was originally established as a wildlife preserve for the breeding of endangered North American animals. However, changes forced by Congress resulted in the zoo becoming more of a public park, with only limited space allocated for wildlife. Still, the mission of the

Terry L. Maple in 1978 with a baby orangutan at the Yerkes Primate Research Center of Emory University. Orangutans from Yerkes have been housed at the zoo for more than twenty-five years.
(Photograph by Frank Kiernan)

park ("for the advancement of science and the instruction and recreation of the people") was a solid, conservationist vision, and it ensured a century of leadership within the zoo world. In 1886, the New York Zoological Society founded its famed Bronx Zoo, declaring three major objectives. First, the founders proclaimed, they would build a zoological park along lines never before attempted—they would be truly innovative, placing animals in natural surroundings, and in free-range large enclosures rather than small paddocks and cages. Second, they would be dedicated to the promotion of zoology. And third, they would be devoted to the preservation of native animals. These plans were truly progressive, predating by some eighty years the "landscape immersion" movement that started in the 1970s. Sadly, the origins of most American zoos were less than noble, and most of the creatures populating our first zoos were prisoners in dreadful, cramped cages, victims to the taunting of an uninformed, insensitive public. Zoos and menageries were pretty much the same thing at the turn of this century.

Atlanta's zoo, too, was born without vision, without plans, without hopes, and nearly 100 years passed before it found a place on the zoo world stage. It was a collection without a cause and without a public leader. In fact, the local menagerie in Grant Park was so invisible that one of Atlanta's most prominent families, the first family of Coca-Cola, the Candlers, decided to build a zoo of their own on Briarcliff road near Emory University. According to Mettelen Thompson Moore (Graham and Roberts, 1992):

> PaPa decided that the children of Atlanta didn't have a zoo, and that they needed one. So he commissioned a curator to go to Europe and Africa and get more animals to go with the ones he already had. . . . He came back and drew up the plans for the zoo to fit in the front yard at Briarcliff.

The only public development even remotely related to a vision in those early days was the creation of the park in which the Grant Park Zoo animals would be located. Built on land that local philanthropist Sidney Root persuaded railroad magnate Lemuel Pratt Grant to donate to the city, it was Atlanta's first public park. Although Atlanta was a small city at the time, some of its leaders embraced the idea of landscape architect Frederick Law Olmsted to provide oases of green within the urban, concrete metropolis. The Atlanta Park Commission labeled Grant Park the "lungs of the city," a place where people could go to "mend broken health with pure air, to elevate their minds with the beauties of nature and art, to meet with one another in social gatherings . . . to strengthen mind and body for another week of labor." To the extent that the small animal collection fit that concept, then, it benefited from a certain vision, but even the goals for the park were to be completely neglected in coming years.

From time to time, newer and bigger facilities were added to the Atlanta Zoo in the 1940s, 1950s and 1960s, but each facility fell quickly out of fashion. A new feline house was opened in 1957, a primate house in 1959, new bear grottos in 1961, and a reptile house in 1967, but these exhibits were outdated even before they were built, representing, as they did, the glass-fronted, bathroom-tile zoo architecture of the 1950s and early 1960s.

Most of the exhibit spaces were far too small for their inhabitants and bore no relationship to the animals' needs. Nor did they offer much to the visitors, who viewed the animals the way they might view pelts or skeletons in a natural history museum. In addition, the exhibits were organized taxonomically—all big cats in the same building, all primates in another, all reptiles under one roof. While this gave the visitor some understanding of the diversity within different families of animals, it bore no relation to the types of habitats and parts of the world these animals truly represented. African lions and jaguars, for instance, live continents apart and inhabit vastly different landscapes.

By the late 1960s and early 1970s, ideas about how animals could be exhibited were beginning to change dramatically. Advances by animal biologists and behaviorists, by scientists studying animals in the wild, and by creative, bold architects were resulting in a dramatic new concept for zoo exhibitry—landscape immersion, where both animals and people explore a habitat modeled after the animals' native lands.

In 1975, I came to Atlanta from California to teach psychology at Emory University and to study the four species of great apes at the esteemed Yerkes Primate Research Center at Emory. On my first day in town, I decided to take a look at the zoo. It was a sunny, cool fall day, and I was primed for a pleasant afternoon, hoping to find some opportunities to study great apes. I discovered a place that was literally falling apart. It was hardly a zoo at all.

Grim and decaying, most of the animal facilities were cramped and inappropriate. The exhibits were repugnant, evoking reflexive sneers and nose holding. Windows were cracking, walls were peeling, and there were no staff members in sight. Visitor services were minimal and unpleasant. A couple of food stands served inedible hot dogs, and the rest rooms were dirty. This was a place fit for neither animals nor people.

In 1970, a group of concerned citizens had formed the Atlanta Zoological Society to help support the zoo, and after a few visits to the zoo, I was recruited to the cause. It was a tiny organization but cocksure in its commitment. I was interested to find that the society was academic in its orientation. In contrast to the zoo itself, the society's professionalism was comforting. And it was this group that began the campaign to give the zoo its long-needed vision. The society's bylaws, written in 1970, reflected its sense of mission:

> The corporation is organized . . . to advance the sciences of zoology and natural history with emphasis upon, but not limited to, research, education, and conservation . . . to assist and cooperate with any and all zoological gardens and parks . . . to sponsor, own, and direct zoological gardens and collections of living animal forms. . . .

Ten years later, the society approved a simple mission statement, but one that was full of hope: "The Atlanta Zoological Society intends to create and operate a zoological garden worthy of international recognition." By this time, a new philosophy about the exhibition of animals was emerging, and the society reflected that new vision as well:

> The Atlanta Zoological Society wants to share with the public the excitement and drama of living creatures . . . a setting of natural habitats and relationships. We want people to share our love of nature and our respect for the majesty of wildlife. Our visitors . . . should feel their visit has been a special opportunity to be the invited guest in the animal's world.

As an assistant professor at Emory, I had also enjoyed access to the unique primate collection at the Yerkes Primate Center, which was the real draw in luring me to Atlanta. On my first visit there, I was overwhelmed by the sight and sound of so many apes: more than 40 orangutans, 20 gorillas, and 100 chimpanzees, including the rare "bonobo," or pygmy chimpanzee. As I walked down the corridors, stoic orangs stared at me silently, gorillas beat their enormous chests, and chimpanzees hooted and howled. One chimp chose to fling excrement at me, anointing my coat with a boutonniere that I noticed only after my return to campus. I had been struck by a pithy body of evidence of the species' vast differences in temperament. I knew there was much to learn about these creatures.

The director of Yerkes at the time was Dr. Geoffrey Bourne, one of the genuine "silverbacks" (the term for an adult, male gorilla troop leader) of the academic world. Dr. Bourne was also the founding president of the Atlanta Zoological Society, and he was the person who invited me to join their board of directors. Dr. Bourne had hopes that the society would eventually gain control of the zoo's management, and I wondered whether he envisioned himself as zoo director, even though that would have been a clear demotion at the time. (Years later, as we opened our first natural habitat at the zoo, he confided to me that he had indeed dreamed about becoming a zoo director.)

By 1976, I had become chairman of the society's first research and education committee, commissioned for duty to attack the zoo's many and enduring problems. One of its most glaring shortcomings, and one which I tried to address early on, was the disengagement of the staff from the zoo profession as a whole. This problem became all too clear to me when I attended the 1977 national conference of the American Association of Zoological Parks and Aquariums (AAZPA) in San Diego to lecture about my studies of the Atlanta Zoo orangutans (all of them on loan from Yerkes). I was in the audience when it was announced that the Atlanta Zoo had won a significant achievement award for building public awareness about the endangered indigo snake. I looked around the room and no one stood up. No representative of the Atlanta Zoo was in attendance at this important professional conference. So, I advanced to the podium and sheepishly accepted the award on behalf of the zoo. It should have been a proud moment, but I carried it back to Atlanta with a heavy heart.

The Zoological Society was fighting many battles in those days, with only limited success. In 1976, a $5 million bond issue for renovating the zoo was narrowly defeated. Perhaps if the society had been larger and had had more friends in local government, the city might have made a greater effort to promote the zoo cause. Given this outcome, it seemed reasonable to focus on attracting members. When I left Atlanta on sabbatical in December 1980 to spend a year working with the Audubon Zoo in New Orleans, I was confident that the worm had turned. I returned one year later to find that, in spite of the society's growth and enthusiasm, the situation at the zoo continued to deteriorate. The media was beginning to take note of the zoo's difficulties, especially since the string of child murder cases that had so occupied everyone's attention had seemingly been solved.

By 1983, there was substantial conflict among the zoo staff, reflecting animosity between the zoo director and the veterinarian. The staff became polarized along those lines, with some (largely composed of the members of the mammal department) supporting the zoo veterinarian and others (from the reptile department) still supporting the zoo director (a herpetologist himself). The director's supporters even formed a union to resist the authority of the city bureaucracy, and systematically leaked information to newspaper reporters about accidents and problems at the zoo. The zoo was essentially leaderless now, with only a succession of absentee city managers nominally running things. By the end of the year, the zoo director had resigned and the zoo had been suspended from membership in AAZPA, the zoo world's national association. This action was precipitated by an inspection conducted by three experienced zoo directors. The breakdown of discipline, communication and cohesion among the staff stunned the inspection team. Their report was characterized by harsh words:

> Never have we encountered such an environment of mistrust, anger, and doubt among the top levels of management in any zoo. In fact, it appears that the major concern of the Director and Veterinarian is to prove each other incompetent. . . . In a situation such as this something must suffer—in this case it has clearly been the animals and the overall condition of the zoo.

In spite of the wrenching difficulties of 1983, the Zoological Society continued to lobby for change, commissioning a far-reaching master plan for rebuilding the zoo. The $35 million plan for a natural habitat zoo was revealed to the public in January 1984.

Only a month later, as I was flying to Africa with so many dedicated members, the bomb dropped: our zoo was one of the nation's worst. Deep down inside we all recognized how bad it really was, but we also thought we were on the verge of turning it around. We could never have anticipated the string of crushing events that would occur before our zoo could finally be righted.

Courageously, the leaders of our Zoological Society presented a revised $25 million dollar plan to the city council in March 1984, complete with a strategy for financing it with a variety of bonds, government grants, and private donations, and a management structure by private citizens. "If the zoo is not improved, it could be required to close," wrote Parks commissioner Carolyn Boyd Hatcher. "The zoo has a great opportunity to become an internationally recog-

A jaguar in the old Atlanta Zoo feline house in 1984. The feline house was closed later that year and in 1988 was remodeled to accommodate Willie B. and sixteen gorillas from Yerkes. (Photograph by Richard D. Fowlkes)

nized center for zoological, veterinary and related scientific research," she urged.

It was a good plan, and the society decided to proceed with fund-raising, even while the plan was being considered by the city. A few weeks later, the society learned that the zoo's ailing elephant, Twinkles, had died, while supposedly resting and recovering at a farm near Alpharetta. A week later, the public and the members of the zoo society learned that the ailing elephant had in fact been turned over to a traveling circus in North Carolina, where it died.

That was just the beginning of many animal and management horror stories that would hit the newspapers week after week. Newspaper reports mentioned prairie dog burrows mistakenly plugged with cement, mysterious deaths of several old cats and bears, and the selling and eating of surplus rabbits from the children's zoo. By early June, Commissioner Hatcher recommended that zoo veterinarian Dr. Emmett Ashley take a leave of absence, which he did, amid charges of questionable animal care and management. Atlanta mayor Andrew Young launched a full-scale investigation by the city's law department, and other investigators from the Humane Society of the United States and the U.S. Department of Agriculture began to descend on the zoo.

On June 1, 1984, in the midst of this imbroglio, I received an urgent phone call from city hall. Mayor Andrew Young was assembling a select group of local and national leaders for a meeting to discuss the deepening zoo crisis. I felt proud that I had been asked to help. The zoo's biggest liability was all too clear, I thought: a lack of strong leadership.

There was plenty of expertise available at the meeting on that day. There were primate experts, animal welfare specialists, veterinarians, representatives of humane societies, members of the zoological society, the USDA, and city bureaucrats from the law department to the parks department. Mayor Young explained that the zoo's problem was a polarized power struggle between the reptile keepers and the mammal keepers, who were locked in a nasty and protracted battle. His analysis was all too familiar. I knew the problems were much deeper than that, but I could also place this confrontation in another time and context, in another, very distant place. I thought of British naturalist Alfred Russel Wallace's description of the orangutan (which he called the Mawas) and the crocodile locked in combat in the jungles of Borneo:

> No animal is strong enough to hurt the Mawas, and the only creature he ever fights with is the crocodile. . . . He always kills the crocodile by main strength, standing upon it, pulling open its jaws, and ripping up its throat. . . .
>
> *The Malay Archipelago*

This image sustained me as I considered whether Wallace's illustration of this epic struggle for existence would be an appropriate logo for our troubled zoo.

But the mayor was right about one thing: the zoo was out of control and no bureaucrat from city hall had been able to put it right. The group spoke up loud and clear. The zoo could not be saved, they said, without strong and able zoological leadership. "Furthermore," they opined, "this leader must be hired immediately, on an interim basis if necessary." I had heard that a leader might be recruited from within the room, at that very meeting, but I was stunned when the group turned to me.

Cautiously, I agreed to consider the assignment. "If my conditions can be met," I said, reasoning quickly, "perhaps I could find a way to get the job done." I knew that I had a unique advantage, since summer break was near and I had cleared my schedule for those three months anyway. Everyone agreed that the decision would be kept confidential until the details could be resolved, but by the time I got back to my office at Georgia Tech my name had already been leaked. A television crew was waiting at my door. They wanted an interview for the 6 o'clock news. I knew then that there was no turning back. The zoo's problems were now *my* problems, and the entire city was about to find out.

I had less than a year of zoo management training under my belt, acquired at the Audubon Zoo, and I had served for four years on the board of the Atlanta Zoological Society. That was the sum total of my management experience for the job. But I was tapped because no credentialed zoo director would have taken the Atlanta Zoo job at this moment in its volatile history. I was unproven as an administrator, but I was not unqualified. My background in animal behavior and my reputation as a professor (now at Georgia Tech) would give me credibility, I hoped, and I could use my three-month period of service to negotiate for some of the immediate changes I thought were necessary for the zoo to change direction.

On June 6, 1984, Mayor Young scheduled a press con-

A gorilla reaches for a handout from her cage in the old Audubon Zoo in 1976. This zoo was completely rebuilt during the 1980s and is now regarded as one of the ten best zoos in America. (Photograph by Terry L. Maple)

ference to announce my appointment. The mayor prepared me for the ordeal by recalling the occasion when he was so intimidated by the press that he resigned his position at the United Nations. He vowed that he would never allow them to intimidate him again. In that moment of candor, he gave me strength and confidence, and I believed that, with the mayor's support, I would be successful. I did my best to exude optimism when I stepped forward and faced the largest crowd of reporters I could possibly have imagined. I realized at that moment just how much interest there was in the zoo, and I knew that if it could be channeled and utilized properly, we could obtain the public support we would need finally to rebuild it.

And sure enough, there was an almost immediate shift in attitude. The stories that came out the next day were positive and optimistic: a Georgia Tech professor, an expert in animal welfare, would take over the zoo and begin to fix it. "From the ashes we will build a better zoo," I said at the time.

I went back to the zoo and took up residence in a tiny wooden building on the grounds. There were only thirty paid staff, and a woefully inadequate budget, to care for a modest collection of about 1,000 animals, most of them reptiles. The city council had to fund the position at step seven of the pay range ($37,239.80) just to match my modest professor's salary! Still, I knew that I had a lot of leverage to make things happen, and I quickly decided on three immediate priorities: a direct reporting relationship to the parks commissioner, an administrative assistant who understood city procedures, and administrative action that would immediately correct the veterinary situation. Commissioner Hatcher, a former biology teacher, made all three priorities a reality, and I was immediately empowered to address longstanding problems. The first big step was to hire a new veterinarian from the prestigious University of California at Davis, Dr. Rita McManamon. In transition, the Yerkes Primate Center agreed to loan the zoo its chief veterinarian, Dr. Brent

Swenson, who agreed to look after the collection until the new, full-time veterinarian was on board.

But not all problems could be solved this quickly. After just four weeks on the job, my leadership was tested when our young giraffe, Daisy, went into labor unexpectedly. Giraffe births, especially first ones, are no easy endeavor. Daisy labored many hours with a breech birth, and it soon became obvious that it was a stillborn calf, and that Daisy herself would require surgery in order to survive. Since we had no surgical facilities at the zoo, we decided to transport the giraffe to the University of Georgia veterinary school in Athens. Transporting a giraffe is difficult even under the best of circumstances. We did not have an adequate transport crate, so the staff spent the next few hours desperately constructing one. Finally, the crate was finished, the giraffe loaded in, and the crate put onto a flatbed truck. The staff began the 65-mile drive to Athens early in the evening, encountered severe thunder and lightning along the way, and did not reach Athens until after midnight. The complicated surgery went well, however, and our keepers elected to bring Daisy back to the zoo early the next morning. But on the drive back, just a few miles away from the zoo, Daisy died, a victim of stress and prolonged anesthesia. To make matters worse, the rickety truck and crate had hit some overhead utility wires en route to the zoo, and local police had arrived to deal with the emergency. The media, through their monitoring of police activities, found out about the tragedy even before I had been briefed on the details.

I tried to collect my thoughts. I was proud of the staff's spirit and the teamwork they exhibited under the worst of conditions. I was grateful for the expertise of the surgeons in Athens. And I was angry—angry over the dilapidated facilities, the lack of preparation for this birth, our inability to respond quickly with proper care. Still, these were the cards we had been dealt. We had to work with what we had. I resolved to deal with the situation openly. We had tried hard. We had failed. Next time it would be better. I could only hope that the media, and the public, would see it that way. If not, our reform administration might meet a quick end.

All day and into the night, I met with reporters from newspapers, radio, and television, facing each one individually and taking as much time as needed, giving out all the details and information I had, letting them see my frustration and my determination. When the reports began to appear, they were sympathetic, and they were accurate. We had done our best in a difficult situation, the media concluded. A report in the *Atlanta Constitution*, for example, mentioned the death of Twinkles and other recent problems at the zoo but then offered the qualification that "giraffes are notoriously delicate animals." We were being treated fairly by the press, and this was a big step forward for the zoo.

Not long afterward, a reporter who had previously skewered the zoo in a series of stories called for an in-depth interview. The story that appeared the following day was mildly critical and suffered from a fair number of inaccuracies. I was inclined to ignore it, but my staff was quite upset. They told me that I should not let the errors stand. So I sent the newspaper a detailed critique of the piece. To my surprise, my letter was prominently published, together with my most flattering file photograph. That investigative reporter never again wrote about the zoo. Perhaps the editors had turned the corner, too, and were ready to give their poor zoo at least the benefit of the doubt. From that day forward, I never met an antagonistic reporter. They had done their job exposing the zoo crisis; now it was time to document our transition to excellence.

While I served as interim director, a formal search continued for a permanent director. Commissioner Hatcher added my name to the candidate list, which was still very limited. In fact, the leading candidates were friends of mine whom I had convinced to at least consider the job, since I was not at all sure at first that I would want to stay. However, I did, finally, interview for the permanent position, with the stipulation that, if selected, I would serve on a year-to-year basis, since I would have to reapply each year for leave from Georgia Tech. Commissioner Hatcher asked me to accept the "permanent" appointment in September 1984, one week before that year's AAZPA meeting in Miami.

With Dr. McManamon on board, and leadership stability, I began to look to the best zoos around the country for additional help. Actually, I began to look to them for staff, and quickly recruited (some would say "stole") a number of highly qualified individuals from some fine zoos, including Dr. C. Dietrich Schaaf, who left the Philadelphia Zoo to lead our animal management division.

It wasn't easy to woo talent to Atlanta. The zoo's troubles had been national news, so potential staff had to be convinced that we were truly on the road to recovery. In his first interview with the press after joining us as general curator, Dr. Schaaf gave testimony to this personal, hard-sell approach: "I told [Dr. Maple] very frankly that if I'd seen an advertisement for the position in a professional newsletter, I wouldn't have looked twice because of the difficulties that they had here."

We were astonishingly successful in the daunting task of recruiting the best zoological talent to our small zoo. In addition to Dr. McManamon and Dr. Schaaf, we landed Rich Block and then Jeff Swanagan from the Columbus Zoo to head up our education department. We recruited mammal curators John Croxton and Tony Vecchio from the respected Riverbanks Zoo and Sam Winslow from the Audubon Zoo in New Orleans. Guy Farnell and John Fowler, our first and only bird curators, came from the Audubon Zoo as well, and I was later especially pleased to rob scientific staff from the acclaimed Los Angeles and National zoos—Dr. Debra Forthman and Dr. Elizabeth Stevens, respectively. This caliber of talent made all the difference in our advance to respectability.

We had turned the corner. We still had many immediate

The Atlanta Zoo's reptile collection was its lone outstanding feature in June 1984. (Photograph by Richard D. Fowlkes)

problems to address, but we could start thinking in earnest about the future, about what the zoo could become, and what it could give back to the community. We could start thinking about what we wanted to do, rather than undo. We could start making the zoo a pleasant, fun place to visit and to work in. As I collected my staff, little by little, I vowed to manage them the way Ed Loveland, my department chairman had managed his faculty at Georgia Tech: by encouraging and mentoring, by providing support and resources, getting people together for a beer after a stressful day, and enjoying the fun moments that occurred during our many struggles. I vowed to work with our staff to build a zoo that would accomplish great things. Fortunately, I was being managed well, too; with Carolyn Hatcher and Bob Petty in control of the community, I was free to concentrate on managing the zoo.

The new year, 1985, started off with a sense of purpose and growing unity at the zoo. By the end of the year, the city and county announced that they had approved the money for rebuilding the zoo, $16 million in bonds, as well as more than $5 million in operating expenses for the next seven years. The name of the zoo was changed to "Zoo Atlanta," reflecting its reversal of fortune. The Zoological Society set to work to raise an additional $9 million in capital funds. In October, the new Zoo Atlanta management plan was officially announced, including the transfer of control from the city to a new nonprofit governing board composed of Atlanta's top business leaders. Robert M. Holder, Jr., of Holder Corporation, became Zoo Atlanta's founding chairman.

A veterinary clinic opened at the zoo in November, and some animals were moved to other zoos to provide more space for those that remained. Round-the-clock security was added, the maintenance crew was expanded, and Lorraine Perkins, the first dedicated registrar in the zoo's history, brought the animal records up to a standard of excellence. Three keepers won national awards that year, and the Humane Society of the United States stated publicly that the zoo had changed considerably for the better. The renowned landscape design firm Coe & Lee Associates (now Coe, Lee, Robinson and Roesch) came on board to update the 1983 concept plan and began working on innovative, far-reaching ideas for new exhibits. And, the Ford Motor Company provided our first big donation, $100,000, to help build a world-class gorilla exhibit, the first installment in what would become a multimillion dollar gift to the zoo. A plethora of problems remained, but we had come a very long way.

During that first year I spoke to almost every civic organization in Atlanta, trying to express our commitment to building a better zoo. Somewhere along the line, the words "The World's Next Great Zoo" slipped off my tongue, and they were appropriate. Zoo Atlanta would indeed become part of, and even a leader in, a powerful zoo revolution.

CHARISMATIC MEGAVERTEBRATES AND OTHER ZOO TALES

Picasso . . . was visited by a journalist who asked him what he thought of the chimpanzee painting. Picasso disappeared from the room, then suddenly reappeared, his arms swinging low, leaped at the reporter, and bit him. In his own way, he seemed to be saying that the ape and he were artists in common.

***Desmond Morris,* Animal Days**

The revolutionary changes that have occurred in zoos during the past fifteen or twenty years are based on many decades of learning about animals, on many scientific studies undertaken by psychologists, biologists, ethologists, field scientists, and others. Zoo Atlanta's turnaround, and the massive re-creations at other zoos, could not have taken place without this foundation of knowledge. A review of zoo history, as well as the evolving scientific study of animal behavior, will help explain how our approach to natural zoo environments has been shaped and how Zoo Atlanta is part of the larger zoo revolution.

Zoos, of sorts, began as far back as 2500 B.C., when Egyptian rulers experimented with keeping a variety of hoofstock and other wild animals. Ancient Chinese royalty maintained menageries of beasts from their fertile lands.

The ancient Greeks, like Aristotle, kept collections of wild animals brought back by army expeditions, and the ancient Romans acquired huge collections of lions, tigers, elephants, and other wild species from their exploits, using many of them in their warlike gladiator games. Medieval nobility also often kept collections of exotic animals. Most of these "zoos," however, were the private domains of the ruling classes.

Zoos became firmly established as public gathering places in the late eighteenth and early nineteenth centuries. The Paris Zoo opened in 1793, followed by zoos in London (1826), Amsterdam (1838), Berlin (1848), and Antwerp (1848). In the United States, the Central Park Zoo opened in 1873, followed by the Philadelphia Zoo in 1874. A number of other American zoos were opened during the late 1800s, including Atlanta's in 1889. During this time, zoos were beginning to see themselves as providing educa-

A WSB television crew records orphaned African elephants as their human caretakers teach them to bathe in mud. At the center of the photograph are Zoo Atlanta's lead elephant keeper, Jim Black, and elephant advocate Daphne Sheldrick. (Photograph by Terry L. Maple)

tion in natural history, and many of their founders expressed a vision extolling science, education, and recreation. No longer the private domain of royalty, zoos in this epoch invited the "masses" to experience the joys of a living collection.

Yet, while zoos were well established in the world by the nineteenth century, most of the exotic animals on exhibit were poorly understood. Explorers and hunters captured strange creatures on trips to the wild, and zookeepers placed them in zoo cages with little knowledge of their natures or the habitats they came from. The gorilla is "an impossible piece of hideousness . . . as awful as a nightmare dream," wrote hunter Paul Du Chaillu in the 1860s. The movie gorilla King Kong represented the state of public understanding at the time this film was released. So, when confronted with gorillas and other strange creatures in a zoo, all visitors could do was gawk. People were confused by them, and feared them.

Nowadays, large, exciting animals like the gorilla, the elephant, and the lion are known as "charismatic megavertebrates." Conservationists see these creatures with charisma as the key to attracting support for conservation, since people simply are more interested in them. In East Africa, photographic safaris are not considered successful unless the patrons have observed the "big five": elephant, rhino, buffalo, lion, and leopard. In my opinion, cheetahs, baboons, zebras, and ostriches are charismatic, too, but to some degree "charisma" depends on the eye of the beholder. Clare Richardson, Zoo Atlanta's executive vice-president for marketing and development, dares to classify the zoo director as a "charismatic megavertebrate." So far, she has diplomatically refused to specify whether it is my personality or great size that qualifies me for membership.

Today, we know these animals so much better. But that knowledge did not come easily or quickly. Scientific study of some of the animals that we exhibited in our zoos was the first step, although many of these studies were undertaken only for insight into human behavior and evolution. Some of the earliest zoo studies, for example, were conducted by psychologists Harry F. Harlow and his graduate student Abraham Maslow, starting in the 1930s. (Coincidentally, Harlow was the adviser of my own graduate school adviser—Gary Mitchell—and thus a kind of academic grandfather to me.) Harlow was interested in investigating the variables associated with attachment, affection, and successful social interaction, and together with Maslow, studied the sexual and aggressive behaviors of rhesus monkeys in the zoo. (Maslow later went on to expand on these themes in his stewardship of the human potential movement.) Harlow and Maslow conducted this research at the tiny Vilas Park Zoo in Madison, Wisconsin, only because their university had no animal laboratory at the time. A few years later, Maslow made additional observations on monkeys living at the Bronx Zoo. Although these studies were intended for use in understanding human psychology, they also served as a foundation for our knowledge and study of zoo animals. Still, zoos at the time did not make the connection between this work and the conditions that affected the animals living there. (For further information on Maslow and Harlow, see my historical chapter in *Captivity and Behavior*, 1979.)

At the same time Harlow was formulating his ideas, developmental psychologists were studying early patterns of attachment in humans, and clinical psychologists were observing the profound effects of isolation and social deprivation among disturbed children and adults in psychiatric hospitals. Studies of animals occurred here, too. In addition, anthropologists working with developing cultures and with nonhuman primates in the wild were learning more about social development and the variables that control it.

A few scientists may be regarded as early pioneers in the psychological study of the nonhuman primates. C. Ray Carpenter (who happened to be a Stanford University classmate of Harlow) began an important study at the San

Diego Zoo in 1937. His subjects were the rare mountain gorillas residing there, a species that was a virtual mystery at the time. Carpenter gathered important data about the gorillas' locomotor, grooming, play, and expressive behaviors and also documented instances of what he felt were acts of intelligence and cooperation.

Carpenter was just one of several successful protégés of Robert M. Yerkes, who was perhaps the finest comparative psychologist of his time. Yerkes' early studies of primates really uncovered most of the basic information about them. One of his most interesting publications was a 1925 book entitled *Almost Human*. In this book, Yerkes tells the story of a woman, Madame Rosalia Abreu, who had a colony of primates in Cuba. Through her success in housing and breeding these animals, Yerkes was able to gain a clear understanding of the environmental variables that affect primates in captivity, and to determine the major conditions needed for their well-being.

The work of Konrad Lorenz, beginning in the 1930s, added a whole new dimension to our understanding of animals. Until I read the works of Lorenz, I believed (in the tradition of psychologist B. F. Skinner) that most animal and human behavior could be explained by the laws of learning. Lorenz's book *On Aggression* made me begin to think of behavior in a very different way—from a biological approach. For example, Lorenz believed that aggression was not an aberrant behavior but a normal, biological response, a part of any organism's repertoire of innate behaviors. People and animals both ritualize their fighting—as when men stare, clench fists, and gesticulate before sparring—and cease attacking when their opponent shows signals of appeasement.

Lorenz's ideas were compelling, and I became enamored of this new science, called "ethology," or the biological approach to studying animal behavior. The dominant methodology of ethologists consisted of naturalistic observations, which were used to generate descriptive data.

Ethologists studied animals as animals, regardless of whether the work had any application to humans. They focused at first on simple behaviors in reasonably simple organisms, such as insects, fish, and birds. Ethologists began to include monkeys and apes in their studies just about the time I entered graduate school, in the late 1960s. A series of readings I put together for a seminar on aggression became my first book, called *Aggression, Hostility, and Violence* (edited with the assistance of my teacher Doug Matheson). By 1973, Lorenz, along with Niko Tinbergen and Karl Von Frisch, had won the Nobel Prize for physiology and medicine, and ethology was a bonafide scientific movement.

Other great advances in animal studies came through the work of field biologists and anthropologists studying in the wild, such as George Schaller, Jane Goodall, and Dian Fossey, beginning in the late 1950s. (Surprisingly, the earliest field studies of nonhuman primates had been conducted in the 1930s and 1940s by psychologists Harold Bingham, Henry Nissan, and C. Ray Carpenter.) These scientists were bringing back details about the life of these animals in the wild, and I was delighted to be Jane Goodall's guide when she visited our lab at the University of California at Davis. I was especially eager to tell her about some experiments that I was starting on interspecies social behavior, since I had studied her reports about conflicts between baboons and chimpanzees at her field site in Tanzania. I was just beginning to learn all about baboons and had recently obtained an adult female to study. I had been told that she was a "yellow baboon," even though she had a distinctly green coat. When I showed this baboon to Dr. Goodall, she informed me that it was an infant "olive baboon." I was chagrined, but it was just one of a myriad of things I and so many others have learned from Goodall. Later in my career, I was privileged to visit her in Tanzania, and to discuss with her my new ideas on improving captive housing conditions for chimpanzees.

Thankfully, my early ignorance of baboon taxonomy was not held against me.

While scientists were learning a lot about animals during the next decade, this knowledge seemed to have almost no influence on the way zoos managed their animals. In my college and graduate research, I had uncovered only two practicing "zoo psychologists": Dr. Hal Markowitz, at that time research director for the Portland, Oregon, Zoo, and

Professor Heini Hediger (Photograph by Dr. Christian Schmidt)

the late Dr. Heini Hediger, then emeritus director of Zoo Zürich in Switzerland.

Now a professor at San Francisco State, Markowitz developed innovative techniques that have been labeled "behavioral enrichment." What he did was provide captive animals with new, specially designed activities and environments and then study the results. His work was a reaction to the sterile environments of zoos and to the low activity of many of the animals; as such it provided pioneering techniques giving captive animals greater control over events in their lives. He succeeded admirably. Examples of his techniques included showers that could be activated by elephants, vertical pathways for gibbons, mechanical prey for big cats that produced a treat after capture, and even meatballs that flew through the air to stimulate prey-catching behaviors. Mandrill baboons could engage their brains by playing tic-tac-toe and reaction-time games with the public. The baboons usually won, and the public loved every minute of it. Markowitz described the reasoning behind one of these projects:

> Without a large budget it was impossible to provide a forest for gibbons with appropriate climactic conditions. The first of our major behaviorally engineered exhibits demonstrated, however, that it was possible to encourage brachiation [hand-over-hand swinging locomotion] and "flying" around the cage while simultaneously providing the animals some entertainment and control over their own feeding.
>
> (*Behavioral Enrichment in the Zoo*)

I had read the English editions of Heini Hediger's classic works early in my career. He was the most published zoo director of all time, with more than 300 publications to his credit, and I fell under the spell of his scholarly influence. His perspective was thoroughly scientific, since he was a professor of ethology at the University of Zürich while he served as zoo director. Hediger brought the two institutions together to the benefit of each. As a young man he had also conducted field studies in Africa and the South Pacific. In 1937 he became director of Bern's Dahjholzli Zoo and was appointed director of Zoo Zürich ten years later. Here he was best known for developing the zoo's "Africa House" in 1965, where he applied his knowledge of the animals' natural history, behavioral proclivities, and responses to captivity. This exhibit simulated conditions in the wild like no other before or since. Hediger also helped pioneer the concept of "zoo biology," or the scientific study of animals and everything else in the zoo. His efforts dramatically advanced understanding of animals and zoos at a crucial time, and played a role in the redevelopment of Zoo Atlanta and other zoos.

My own firsthand scientific study of animals began at the California Primate Research Center. But my interests in primate behavior also led me to the nearest zoo: the tiny, fifteen-acre Sacramento Zoo, whose director, Bill Meeker, encouraged my studies, allowed me full access to the animals, and made me feel like a real zoo insider. My first memorable encounter occurred one morning as I stood alone in front of the orangutan exhibit. The female was methodically stuffing an old rag into her cavernous mouth, and it struck me that this was a rather peculiar habit. As I stood observing, her gaze slowly shifted toward me. Intuitively, I prepared myself for some sort of communication. She then expertly spit out her wad of cloth, grabbed it with her mammoth hand, tossed it up into the air a few times, and lobbed it, underhand, straight at me. I caught it and threw it back, starting a game of catch that lasted for several minutes, ending only when her toss evaded my grasp and the rag landed in a shrub that neither ape nor man could reach. I knew then that orangutans would teach me a thing or two.

In my first formal zoo study, I observed the social relationships among spider and cebus monkeys at the

Sacramento Zoo. These long-tailed primates are native to the rain forests of Central and South America, a rapidly disappearing habitat. At the Sacramento Zoo, three adult spider monkeys lived on a small, moated island with about twenty cebus monkeys of various ages. This created a bizarre social system, in which the two species developed unusual patterns of interaction, patterns that served no obvious purpose and had no relationship to their behavior in the wild. For example, the spider monkeys frequently offered piggyback rides to the smaller cebus monkeys, who routinely accepted and were carried around the perimeter of the island.

The Sacramento Zoo, like most zoos at that time, was just beginning to learn how to apply knowledge about animal behavior to its animals in the zoo. Many animals lived in inappropriate social situations and developed unusual, even destructive behaviors. Gorillas were housed in monogamous pairs, for example, when in the wild they live in polygamous groups with one dominant male and various females. Understandably, apes at the zoo were not reproducing very well. Since the zoo staff wanted to rectify that situation, they asked me to assist with the problem.

I had recently discovered an obscure film by Swiss primatologist Jörg Hess, which documented examples of gorilla sexual behavior gleaned from experiences at the Basel Zoo. This film provided many of the answers we were looking for, and we decided to share the film with the gorillas. So, for several nights, director Meeker and I projected the film onto the moat wall in the gorilla exhibit, wondering whether the gorillas would watch. They did, and with considerable interest, often carefully touching the wall, trying to make contact with the filmed gorillas, and then sniffing their fingers, which is the way gorillas investigate any novel stimulus. Of course, we never thought that the gorillas could actually learn reproductive skills by watching the film. But we did hope that the change in their routine would at least create some new activity for them, activity that might then lead to social, and even sexual, contact.

The local media were thrilled with our unusual experiment, but, alas, the gorillas never mated. We were pleased to notice, however, that the orangutans also watched, from their enclosure next door, and soon had an offspring of their own. Perhaps the astute orangutans had paid more attention than the gorillas during the "climactic" moments of the film.

I enjoyed these studies of captive animals, but my own experiences soon proved to me that you can never truly know an animal until you examine its natural habitat, until you have encountered it within its own territory. And, in the end, it was this understanding of animals in their wild habitats that had the most to offer the zoo. I had dreamed about Africa—perhaps the greatest continent on earth for viewing exotic wildlife—ever since I could remember. My mother was a fanatic about exotic artifacts and foreign lands, and together we devoured Hollywood's entire repertoire of jungle movies. I recognized the films' excesses even then, but envisioned myself in the bush nevertheless, making contact with wild animals. I had no interest in killing animals, even though my older brother hunted jackrabbits and squirrels in the San Diego hills. I was content instead to collect horned lizards and scour the sky for hawks. I yearned to know what it was like to be one of these animals, to think, feel, and be a wild creature.

I first traveled to Africa in the spring of 1977, at the invitation of a colleague who was living in the Mikumi National Park in Tanzania. When the plane touched down in Dar es Salaam, I was overwhelmed with emotion—I was about to confront my fantasies. As we taxied toward the terminal I could see the lush green vegetation everywhere and began to wonder whether I would learn to survive in this world. My friend Bruce Westlund drove us the long and dusty way to Mikumi, on a two-lane highway packed with little cars, crowded buses, and huge trucks jockeying for position. Most of them spewed dark, diesel smoke, and

The view from Sumatra's Alas River during the taping of WSB's "Search for the Red Ape" in 1988. This trip was the author's first opportunity to observe orangutans in the wild. (Photograph by Terry L. Maple)

pedestrians lined the roadside. It was my first experience with the human side of Africa. Our first stop in Bruce's little village was at an open market, where I learned about bargaining and bartering.

Oddly enough, my first real encounters with wildlife came during trips to the toilet and shower facilities, about thirty paces from our corrugated steel hut. Wild elephants, which seemed to graze and browse comfortably among the people, were numerous in the village. They were particularly fond of the toilet, where they could obtain water, and sooner or later they would uproot the pipes. Understanding the risk, I vowed not to visit the toilet at night, where I might run into the still-active elephants. All night long, I could smell them, and hear them breathing heavily, belching and passing gas as they ripped and chewed the turf. When they were very close to our hut, the walls would tremble as the great beasts rubbed themselves against the corrugated steel.

As I lay in my room at night, alive with geckos, I was learning an important lesson about elephants—they are very active at night. What a contrast, I thought, to an elephant's lot in captivity. In most zoos, elephants were chained at night, unable to move and certainly unable to forage. Zoos did this to prevent the elephants from fighting when the keepers were not there. Now, fifteen years later, we at zoos know how elephants live in the wild, and our captive elephants are no longer chained. We've studied the nocturnal habits of Zoo Atlanta's young elephants, discovering that their frequent aggressive outbursts are a frisky, playful type of sparring. They fight, but they don't get hurt.

While in Africa, I conjured up another way to encourage nocturnal activity in large mammals. In the near future, we hope to build a restaurant at the zoo based on the "tree hotel" concept. In Kenya there are three such hotels—Treetops, The Ark, and the Mountain Lodge—all located in the heavily forested Aberdares National Park, in the shadow of Mount Kenya. Each of them is situated near a waterhole and visitors are encouraged to watch the animals who arrive throughout the night. Our "treetops restaurant" would provide for evening dining around a waterhole and nocturnal activity by elephants, rhinos, hippos, lions, and hyenas. In this way, we can provide evening revenues from dining and party rentals, plus make it economically feasible for some of our animals to be active during the night.

I know of one zoo, the Open Zoo in Singapore, which is experimenting with night animal viewing of elephants, rhinos, and fishing cats. At the annual meeting of the International Union of Directors of Zoological Gardens in 1991, I witnessed the fishing cats in action, and it was an incredible display of natural behavior in nocturnal animals. The more that we learn about the habits of wild animals, the more zoos must change to accommodate their needs.

Tanzania taught other lessons as well. I walked among 100 baboons and gained a fuller appreciation for primate parenting. Mother baboons maintained close contact with their offspring, while the little ones were allowed to engage actively in exploration. Both mothers and offspring were very active, in fact, all day long. They foraged for grasses, flowers, fruits, and insects, covering great distances in their search for food, comfort, and security. At night they ascended trees as a troop, to avoid the fearsome leopards. They remained vigilant, however, and the night was punctuated by their cries. The close mother-child bond was something I would always remember later, when I saw isolated animals in zoos, when we designed new primate exhibits in Atlanta, and even when my wife and I began to have our own children.

I also encountered large herds of antelope, located unique and colorful birds, and constantly examined the ground for insects and reptiles. Birds were especially diverse—more than 1,000 species occur in Kenya alone—and I became a birder right then and there. Life was all around me, and I was learning to observe in new ways. For instance, one has to move slowly, quietly, and patiently to see African wildlife. Even the smallest creatures were teachers. But there were dangers, too. One day, while walking with baboons, we encountered a female elephant with calf. In Tanzania, animal behaviorists must be accompanied by an armed guard or carry arms themselves, and on this day I happened to be carrying the rifle, a .458 single shot relic that hadn't been fired in years. Perhaps the elephant noticed my rifle and thought we were poachers, for she started to chase us. The baboons moved away and we sprinted, but the elephant kept gaining on us. "What now?" I asked Westlund, my experienced colleague. "Head for those trees," he answered. We did, and when we turned to look for the elephant we saw that she had stopped, just about fifty yards from us. She bellowed, flapped her ears, made a few short charges, and then turned away, calf in tow. I figured I was now an expert at recognizing rage in an elephant.

My first opportunity to see great apes in the wild came in 1986 when I traveled with a team from a local television station (WSB-TV) to make a special Zoo Atlanta documentary in Africa and to study wild habitats for inspiration in designing our new exhibits. Our trip took us to several countries, including Rwanda, the home of the mountain gorilla. Just climbing the mountain—which was a real challenge—created a sense of closeness to the animals, as I experienced the exotic vegetation and aromas, the moisture, and the slippery earth. I frequently lost my balance, fell in the mud, and was rewarded with the pain of stinging nettles. But the reward was better than scoring a winning touchdown, better than anything else I had ever experienced in my career.

It isn't possible to adequately describe the emotions that occur when you meet a gorilla face to face, so close you can hear him breathing, surrounded by the peaceful, lush forest. It is a true privilege to be able to live and walk among these magnanimous creatures in their home, and this concept is carefully carried out by the Rwandan guides who lead visitors to see the gorillas. Visitors are taught how to behave—be quiet and nonaggressive, move slowly, keep a certain distance, refrain from touching or making eye contact with the gorillas—and reminded to treat the animals with respect. We were even taught how to make nonthreatening gorilla vocalizations. A loud belch seemed to be the most appropriate form of communication.

Another day, we climbed for hours and there was not a gorilla in sight. When we reached a plateau overlooking a scenic valley, I gave in to exhaustion and sent my Zoo Atlanta colleague, John Fowler, on with the guide. I told them that if I took another step forward, they would have to bury me on the mountain alongside Carl Akeley, the esteemed gorilla advocate who was responsible for the development of this great reserve we were exploring, the Parc des Volcans. As I waited alone on the plateau, I thought about my surroundings, the gorillas' environment, that had so worn me out. Life in the wild is wonderful, but not easy, for animals or for man.

John and the guide returned after two hours, exclaiming excitedly that they had located the gorilla troop. It had been traveling toward the Ugandan border then suddenly, and mysteriously, reversed course and headed back into Rwanda. Miraculously, the troop followed John and the guide almost all the way back to where I was taking my siesta; all I had to do was walk for a few minutes to where they were feeding on some bamboo shoots. "God must want you to see these gorillas," said our guide, laughing. On this most special day, I spent another hour among the gorillas.

Unfortunately, our experience searching for Eastern lowland gorillas in Zaire was not so happy, beginning with our arrival at the airport in Bukavu, an old Belgian town just across Lake Kivu from Rwanda. We were shaken down by guards at the airport, who demanded money for "papers" that were not required. Nevertheless, we managed to "escape" and began our journey into the bush, in Zaire's Kahuzi-Biega National Park. We soon discovered that our guides here did not follow the respectful policies of the Rwandans (although this has since changed for the better). They were very aggressive in tracking gorillas, making lots of noise and carrying firearms. As we entered thick bush, they hacked down the thick vegetation. We discovered a large silverback—a full-grown, male gorilla—after only a short hike. He was feeding peacefully and obliviously until our guides disrupted the scene. We had planned to observe the gorilla unobtrusively, by peeking through the screen of tall bamboo separating us from him. Instead, our guides began to bend back and break the bamboo with a fury, startling the animal. After that, they began to shout at him, provoking the animal until his natural instincts kicked in and he charged us. Fortunately, the gorilla did not sustain his charge, for I felt sure that our guides would have shot him. It was a frightening experience, and we were angered by the ignorance of the guides.

Experiences on other trips to the wild continued to show me how much there was to learn and how many new ideas I could bring back to the zoo. On a television taping expedition down the Alas River in Sumatra, we learned to listen for the ghostly calls of a variety of primates, birds, and insects, as we searched for the elusive orangutan. In time with the complex, melodious calls of gibbons and siamangs, we jumped off the raft and drifted freely down the river in our life jackets, marveling at the tall exotic hardwood trees as we floated peacefully. But it was the sight of a full-grown orangutan, hanging from on high atop the trees, body stretched out and glistening in the morning sun, that touched me the most. Having previously seen orangutans only in sterile zoo environments, I never knew they could look this wonderful.

Aside from their sheer joy and adventure, these trips also provided a multitude of ideas to apply in the zoo. We wanted others to experience some of this magic, rather than observing animals behind bars in sterile cages. We envisioned a setting where people could safely interact with the animals and the landscape, while the animals could live in habitats they really belonged in, and in normal social situations.

Experiences in the wild molded my entire perspective about animal behavior in captivity. I knew at once that this was the model that zoos had to follow, and one we would closely adhere to at Zoo Atlanta. Designers may study other zoo exhibits, but they do better when they study animals in their natural state. Optimal zoo environments needed to look and function like natural habitats in all their wondrous complexity. If we could not replicate nature, at least we could try to simulate it. By approximating nature, we would better the animals' lives in the zoo. After experiencing animals in their own wild, natural environment, I would never be satisfied with the sterility of captivity. I had seen the face of the future zoo, and it was busy, big, green, and good.

My knowledge about animals, especially primates, was significantly enhanced with the birth of our children, and my wife, Addie, and I agreed to apply ideas from my own studies and the work of Harlow and other noted developmental psychologists. My travel in Africa and research for my books on orangutan and gorilla behavior provided additional perspective, as did my interest in the breeding difficulties of great apes in captivity. Many apes in zoos were not reproducing, and the prevailing technique among ape caretakers had been to place newborns into isolated crib units, with no contact except for cleaning and feeding. Very often, their mothers had abandoned or neglected them, dictating intervention and hand-rearing. It was clear to me that we were treating our young apes exactly the way we in the Western world had been raising our own infants. We were placing them in little boxes with toys and blankets, depriving them of the close "contact comfort" that Harlow and others had discovered was fundamentally important to the development of a primate. These apes were also being deprived of

WSB cameraman Roger Herr discovers that Galapagos sea lions have no fear of people. From the television special "Wild, Alive, Endangered." (Photograph by Terry L. Maple)

motion, and of contact with the nipple, which provides relief from stress in addition to nourishment. In my publications, I began to advocate that zoos must try to come closer to this optimal environment of contact for hand-reared infant apes, and ultimately to create environments where apes could live in appropriate social groups. This is something we have achieved at Zoo Atlanta.

I discussed these ideas with my wife as the birth of our first child, Molly, approached. We agreed that the optimal, natural primate environment necessitates a primary caretaker for the baby's early years. The biological model calls for a nursing, doting primate mother, so that is what my wife became. (I, too, doted on Molly but was less available.) We decided that whenever we met up with a problem that we didn't quite know how to solve, we would first think of ourselves as primates and try to come up with a primate-like solution. I labeled this approach "natural parenting." For example, we noticed that if we dined separately from the baby, she would object vociferously. We examined the issue from a primate perspective and concluded that she was upset because we had distanced her. We decided to move her back to our dining table, to be close to us, and to encourage her to experiment with novel sources of food. We then extended this philosophy to dining out, including the baby in these experiences. Here, we also acted like informed primates and brought along little toys and consumable tidbits to occupy her further. Overall, we realized that our little primate needed extensive contact with us, including interaction, stimulation, and enrichment. This meant that Molly accompanied us almost everywhere we went, sometimes, however, making us less than popular visitors.

Two other areas in which we took parental advice from the primates were in providing motion stimulation and in solving sleeping problems. My wife and I were in our mid-thirties when our first child was born, and thus somewhat more sedentary than some younger parents. I noticed that

Molly and our other eventual babies each became very fussy and restless when sitting motionless on my lap, and that they were downright content when I carried them around in a baby backpack, or when they were riding in the car. I understood that this "motion stimulation" was a key component of primate parenting, and that we sedentary adults often tended to deprive our children of it. A "johnny jump-up" for the children and a rocking chair for my wife proved to be excellent solutions to this problem. But there is no substitute for the experience of movement in close contact with parents.

Sleeping provided one of the most telling comparisons between primate infant rearing and our own. Primates always keep their infants close to them, especially when sleeping. Research by anthropologists has shown that in hunter-gatherer societies, babies also remain in constant contact with their mothers. Anthropologist Mel Konner, writing in his 1982 book *The Tangled Wing* about the !Kung bushpeople of southern Africa, noted:

> The dense social context, by providing ample alternative stimulation for both mothers and infant, improves the likelihood that mothers will accept the dependent demands of infants. Paradoxically, this results in decreased proximity seeking and other dependent demands at later ages, except in intensely fear-provoking situations.

Unfortunately, we Westerners have generally been counseled to do the opposite, ignoring our primate needs. Influential psychologist John B. Watson, for example, recommended in 1928 that babies should be treated very strictly, in order that they be weaned from their mothers:

> Mothers just don't know when they kiss their children and pick them up and rock them, caress them and juggle them upon their knee, that they are slowly building up a human being totally unable to cope with a world it must later live in.
>
> (*Psychological Care of Infant and Child*)

Accordingly, Watson advocated that adults should never sleep with their child, and that the child should eat by himself. The child should be put into his room at bedtime, given a pat on the head, and left on his own. "If he howls, let him howl. A week of this regime will give you an orderly bedtime." This approach is the antithesis of "natural parenting."

This point has been amplified in *Breaking the Silence*, by Mariette Hartley, whose grandfather was John Broadus Watson himself:

> My mother's upbringing was purely intellectual. The only time my mother was "kissed on the forehead" was when she was about twelve. . . . Although she was reading the newspaper by the time she was two, there was never any touching, not any at all.
>
> Grandfather's theories infected my mother's life, my life, and the lives of millions.
>
> How do you break a legacy? How do you keep from passing a debilitating inheritance down, generation to generation, like a genetic flaw?

Watson's regime would never work for us, so we committed ourselves to the primate model, letting the babies sleep with us whenever they wanted to. I argued vehemently with pediatricians about this, since they advocated moving a child into her own room after the first few months of life. But I figured that their regimen had been developed for the parents' peace of mind, not for the infant's well-being. Nor did I accept the Skinnerian philosophy which, like Watson's, suggested that retrieving a crying infant reinforces that undesirable behavior. In the primate world, infants cry because they want contact, a natural response to abandonment. Any primate parent who hears its infant crying will quickly retrieve it. By indulging our infants, we do not spoil them or make them dependent. Rather, we do the opposite, providing a safe haven from which to explore novel stimuli. A strong infant-mother bond is the very basis of self-confidence, I think, and primate behavior provides us a wonderful model. When our children grew out of infancy, they were quite content to share their rooms with each other when one of them had problems sleeping alone.

With our children approaching adolescence, we will continue to use the literature of primatology as our textbook, since it served us well during their early years. We hope to understand them better as they begin to distance themselves from us, remembering that this is the way of nature, of biology. It is for them, as it is for any primate, preparation for the independence of adulthood.

TIPS ON "NATURAL PARENTING" AS PRACTICED BY THE APES

1. Keep infants in close contact with parents at all times, and minimize "distancing."
2. Provide infants with motion stimulation; when in contact, stay active.
3. Wherever you go, take the infant along.
4. When an infant cries, for goodness sakes, retrieve the little tot!
5. If he or she awakens in the night, it's okay to take the child to bed, provided that you know how to protect him or her from the sheer weight of the parents.

Understanding primate behavior has helped me in my interactions with human adults as well. In particular, I have had some success observing the nonverbal behaviors of my colleagues, co-workers, friends, and others. I watch closely for any indication of their state of comfort and concern, and even to detect deception. I also try to look at politics through the eyes of a primate. After all, business and politics are governed by laws of behavior. Monkeys, apes, and people often behave in similar ways. At their most quarrelsome extremes, people are like baboons. They posture, bellow, and show their teeth.

Boma the rhinoceros was obtained from the Dvur Kralove Zoo in Czechoslovakia with funds donated by Newt Gingrich. Since black rhinos have a gestation period of twenty-two months, we estimate ours will produce "Olympian" offspring in 1996. (Photograph by Joe Sebo)

Their conflict is mostly bluff. And people, like baboons, form coalitions to get their way. A good baboon watcher understands group behavior in both monkey and humanity.

The gorilla silverback model, for example, can apply to the topic of leadership. Strong leadership by a silverback ensures cooperation and reduces conflict within the group. The same can be said about people. (While gorilla silverbacks are males, I have noticed that among humans, "silverbacks" are increasingly females.) In short, primate behavior helps to explain the everyday life of business and government. Consider the viewpoint of primatologist Frans de Waal, who wrote in his book *Chimpanzee Politics* (1988):

> If we broadly define politics as social manipulation to secure and maintain influential positions, then politics involves every one of us. . . . Chimpanzees . . . are quite blatant about their "baser" motives. Their interest in power is not greater than that of humanity; it is just more obvious. . . . Human beings should regard it as an honour to be classed as political animals.

The *Oxford American Dictionary* defines "charisma" as "the power to inspire devotion and enthusiasm." There is no doubt that big, exotic animals are charismatic in just this way. In fact, the raison d'être of the zoo depends on it. In the zoo, "charismatic megavertebrates" are ambassadors for the entire animal kingdom. The bigger, we assume, the better. Or so I thought.

At the grand opening of the Cecil B. Day Butterfly House, on the grounds of Georgia's magnificent Callaway Gardens, I came face to face with multitudes of charisma, more than a thousand butterflies up close and personal. I was moved by the experience, as were others. I saw so many smiling faces that day, especially on the children who could walk right up to these friendly creatures and, in some cases, make contact with them. (I only wish that we had thought of a butterfly house first; it would be a splendid zoo exhibit!)

Butterflies are grand, proving that a creature doesn't have to be big to be inspiring. Among the butterflies at Callaway Gardens, I was reminded of one that took a liking to me in Sumatra. At midday of a very hot day on the Alas River, a small blue butterfly landed atop my sweaty brow. It stayed with me for nearly an hour, living off my sweat in some meaningful way. I was honored to be a resting place for a small, beautiful creature. On that day, I was inspired by one single blue butterfly.

The more I learn about animals and from animals, the more I recognize the similarities and connections. How wonderful, and sometimes how practical, it has been to be a student of the animals—even to acquire tips on how to be a better parent and a better person. After all, it was Charles Darwin who observed: "He who understands baboon would do more toward metaphysics than Locke." Early on, I believed that one day zoo-goers could take home this sort of understanding—not only factual knowledge about different animals but knowledge of their natural behaviors and social systems, and some framework for understanding them. I also hoped they could take home some of the incredible feelings and thoughts that come from close encounters with animals in the wild. But it would take a new sort of zoo to do that, one which we first would have to figure out how to build.

ARCHITECTS OF THE ARK

Unless one's goal is to learn about the effects of confinement, the educational value of the [hard] zoo is probably more negative than positive. Despite excellent intentions, it is likely that even the best public zoos are creating stereotypes about animal behavior that are not only incorrect but work against the interests of wildlife preservation.

R. Sommer, **Tight Spaces**

It was the same in almost every zoo, and most of us have the same memories. You walked into the "Monkey House," and the first thing that engaged your senses was the smell. "Peeeuuu," screamed the children, as their hands flew up to hold their noses. As you looked at the gorillas, orangutans and monkeys behind glass walls and bars, you instinctively thought of a prison. It didn't help that the ape or monkey in each cage either had his back turned, was picking obsessively at his body, or came lunging and screaming in your direction, banging on the glass and shaking the bars. At first we laughed, self-consciously, then we walked away, some of us disappointed, some of us disquieted, and others of us just filing the experience away with all the other times. That's just the way monkeys are, we said to ourselves.

Of course, it wasn't any better when we got to the Cat House. It smelled even worse, and the cats occupied glass and barred cages that looked pretty much the same as in the Monkey House. But here, the animals never paid any attention to the visitors. They were too busy pacing back and forth in their small spaces. So, we moved on to the outdoor bear grottos. Here we saw a couple of brown bears sleeping on a barren cement landscape, rising only occasionally to look around. There was no shade, and the animals had to retreat to their night dens to escape the midday sun. At such times, the enclosure the public saw looked empty. It was once this way at the Atlanta Zoo, the Central Park Zoo, and zoos in Miami, Dallas, San Francisco, Pittsburgh, and New Orleans, to name just a few.

Yet even these hard exhibits were built with good intentions. Those glass-fronted, blue-tiled monkey cages that looked like empty bathrooms were designed specifically to protect the physical health of the animal. The glass barriers kept human fingers and airborne germs away, preventing the transmission of respiratory and other viruses that monkeys and apes are not able to tolerate well. They also kept visitors from throwing objects that might harm the animal. The tiled floors and bare walls allowed for easy, thorough cleanings, so that no waste, spoiled food, or bacteria could collect and harm the animal. The cages were small enough so that an animal could easily be reached with an anesthetic dart for tranquilizing, in preparation for any medical care needed. But these were the hard exhibits at their best—protecting the physical health of the animals but ignoring their psychological and social needs. At their worst, they did not have even these features, thus exposing their animals to all sorts of harm.

At Zoo Atlanta, gorilla Willie B. II lived in a style common to a typical iron-barred zoo. In fact, the story of Willie B.'s life parallels that of the zoo revolution in many ways. In the late 1950s, a baby gorilla was captured in a tropical forest in west Africa. He was then brought to the United States by an animal trader, who eventually sold him to the Atlanta Zoo, in 1961. Here, a special new cage had been built just for him, a 20' x 40' enclosure, the largest inside the primate house. The enclosure featured a high shelf, a huge tire hanging from a rope, and a long wall of glass in front of strong steel bars, so that many visitors could view him. The young gorilla's arrival in Atlanta was front-page news, and the little animal was given the name Willie B., in honor of the mayor, William B. Hartsfield. (The young gorilla actual-

An orangutan removes some of the landscaping during its first hours in the new enclosure at New Orleans' Audubon Zoo in 1980.
(Photograph by Terry L. Maple)

ly represented the zoo's second attempt at housing this great ape. Willie B. I had arrived in 1959 but survived only until the spring of 1961.) Willie B. II had lots of attention during the years that followed, including special toys and even a television set brought in to amuse him. He was in good physical health, his keepers tended to him with care, and he was a favorite with zoo visitors.

Yet, as Willie B. grew older, it slowly became clear that his life wasn't right. When he wanted to be playful, there was only his rope and his tire, or some other toy. When he wanted to sleep, there was only the hard floor or the shelf. When he wanted to do anything else, there was nothing else to do, except maybe to pick at his dense hair or skin. He grew fatter and fatter from the lack of activity and space. By the late 1970s, with natural habitats beginning to open up at other zoos, Atlanta Zoo visitors began to realize that this was not the best way for a gorilla to live. Some felt sorry for him, while others were bored or annoyed by his lack of activity during the few minutes they spent in front of his cage. Willie wasn't very happy, and neither were his visitors.

One of my teachers in graduate school was Robert Sommer, an esteemed environmental psychologist. It was his conviction that the restrictive architecture seen in most older zoos was dangerous. He cited scholarly studies of mammals in which a whole range of bizarre behaviors developed as adaptations to the isolation and stimulus deprivation. Some of the responses induced by isolation include repetitive pacing, catatonic rocking, self-stimulation and self-mutilation, coprophagia (the consumption of feces), and regurgitation and reingestion of food. Sommer understood that humans in captivity, such as those in prisons and mental hospitals, often engaged in similar behaviors. Accordingly, visiting a "hard zoo" was like visiting a mental ward: the occupants were seen as crazy and self-destructive.

In his book *Tight Spaces*, Sommer describes the effects

of hard architecture on those who must experience it. He identifies its varied attributes as follows:

1. Uniform layout and design
2. Easy and cheap to maintain and clean
3. Surfaces that resist the human imprint
4. Lacks permeability and translucence
5. Maintains order, discipline, and control
6. Perceived as impervious, impersonal, inorganic
7. Encourages passivity and psychic withdrawal

"Soft" architecture, on the other hand, is essentially user-friendly, informal, comfortable, manipulable, variegated, and compelling. Hard zoo architecture is made out of steel, concrete, and tile. It is easy to clean but hard on the animals. The antithesis of hard architecture is a naturalistic landscape. Plants are essentially user-friendly, flexible, complex, and compelling to animals. Soft architecture in the zoo is good for people, too.

Sommer revealed the path for combining my interests in animal behavior, environmental psychology, and zoos, and he encouraged me to discover better ways to house animals in captivity. Further study of the published work of Harlow, Yerkes, Markowitz, and others led me to develop some specific ideas about the social and psychological needs of the great apes, in relation to their life in captivity. But I did not comprehend that it was literally possible to build these animals a new world until, in 1977, I met a young architect by the name of Jon Charles Coe. At that time, Coe was a principal designer for the prominent Seattle architecture firm of Jones and Jones. He and his partners had designed the incredibly innovative gorilla habitat at Seattle's Woodland Park Zoo. Here the Jones and Jones team, working with Seattle zoo director and architect David Hancocks, had developed an exhibit philosophy called "landscape immersion," which would come to revolutionize zoo exhibitry.

I had just returned from my first trip to Africa, where I

walked among the baboons in Tanzania's Mikumi National Park, inspired by the complexity and opportunity inherent in nature. Coe opened the other door for me, demonstrating how architecture could interpret the wild, how it could so well simulate the natural world that it would fool the eyes of even those who had seen animals in the wild. This is exactly what had been accomplished with the new gorilla habitat at the Woodland Park Zoo in Seattle, where they used plants, shrubs, and trees as architectural tools. They built a place so convincing that even sophisticated travelers could not distinguish photographs of the gorillas in Seattle from those of gorillas in west Africa.

Many visitors to the Woodland Park Zoo disliked it at first. In this lush habitat, visitors sometimes had to look hard to find the gorillas, quite unlike the experience of viewing them in traditional cages. Furthermore, some visitors, especially those who had been to the well-manicured San Diego Zoo, complained that the exhibits looked unkept

The Atlanta Zoo once housed five cheetahs in a small cage. The public felt sorry for these creatures, who had no suitable place for running. The animals were eventually surplussed to the St. Louis Zoo and White Oak Plantation to participate in the SSP breeding program.

and overgrown. "Why don't you mow the grass and pull the weeds?" they frequently asked the zoo's director. But gradually, with efforts from the zoo's education and public relations departments, visitors came to enjoy and appreciate the new exhibit. In fact, they had become so used to the natural, free look of the gorillas that it took a few hours before some visitors noticed that, on one occasion, a gorilla had actually escaped the boundaries and was sitting among the visitors themselves.

This natural look was based on a highly sophisticated use of landscape. Today, all of the most important zoo architects are landscape specialists, but Jon Coe was one of the first to make the leap from buildings, which characterized early zoos, to realistic habitat. Some zoos had already adopted an intermediate step, in which formal, park-like lawns and yards were provided for the animals. While these were certainly more natural than indoor or concrete exhibits, they were mainly an aesthetic improvement. They did not necessarily provide behavioral enhancements for the animals, or greater knowledge for the visitors.

Coe was trying actually to re-create the look of the animals' native environment, from its topology to its vegetation. He tried to hide or disguise all reminders of artificiality that might be within view, such as fences and buildings. Sometimes he simply painted these elements in earth tones to make them seem less visible. "Go-away green" was one of his favorite colors, since it blended in with the vegetation.

Coe had more in mind for visitors than just the look of the exhibit, however. He tried to hide or disguise the moats that kept the gorillas in, so that visitors would develop some of the natural excitement, even apprehension, they would feel if they encountered the animal in the wild. He hoped to put the people and animals on a more natural footing with one another, in the open air, without clear barriers, and with gorilla sounds and smells wafting lightly on the breeze. As he often told me, he wanted to "make the hair on the back of your neck stand up." He also believed in positioning the animal exhibits at a higher level than the visitor areas. This way people have to look up at the animals, which he felt would engender greater respect for the animal than did the grottos in old zoos, where visitors peered down at the poor creature in the pit below.

Coe and his colleagues at Jones and Jones had created the finest gorilla facility of its time, and it started me thinking: What else, besides natural and large spaces, does the optimal animal environment require? My own studies revealed that one requirement was to keep the animals in their natural social groupings. In the case of gorillas, for example, this would mean housing them in their natural harem units (with one silverback and several females), and exhibiting them within view of other gorilla troops. I hoped that the first condition would be conducive to breeding and natural socialization, and that the latter condition would stimulate competition, creating a further stimulus for breeding, as well as opportunities for the expression of other normal gorilla behaviors.

I came to understand how these ideal ape exhibits should work, but I didn't have the ability to visualize them, much less to put them on paper in a formal way. When Jon Coe visited Atlanta in 1981 to lecture in my environmental psychology class at Georgia Tech, we shared my latest ideas. As we continued talking, Coe began to sketch, and in one evening he made three conceptual drawings, based on the behavioral propensities of gorillas, chimpanzees, and orangutans.

The gorilla exhibit we envisioned for Zoo Atlanta provided for multiple groups of animals living in contiguous habitats, able to display across the hidden moats. We experienced similar revelations in creating designs for orangutan habitats. These creatures live a semi-solitary life in the wild, and they also spend much of their lives in the canopy of the rain forest, at the tops of ancient trees, stretching their bodies from branch to branch with ease. Even the males reside in trees, despite their greater size and weight. In contrast, an orangutan flattened out on the floor of an old zoo cage does harm to both the animal and its public image. Coe and I created a design for an orangutan exhibit with a network of very tall trees, to provide the vertical space that these apes require. We also designed the exhibit with multiple islands so that males could live separately from females, as they do in the wild, except when the females elected to mate. In our design, a female would be allowed to enter a male's exhibit through a small connecting door or crawlway, but the male would be too large and thus not able to reciprocate. This innovation would simulate an orangutan's life in the wild, where females seek out mature males as breeding partners, spending the rest of their time with offspring or other females.

The experience of creating and conceptualizing with Jon Coe was like a bonfire burning within me. I longed to make these ideas a reality. The exhibits were "crying out" to be built. And, we had the perfect opportunity in Atlanta to obtain the primates to inhabit these exhibits: the Yerkes Primate Center of Emory University. I had already initiated discussions between Yerkes' director Dr. Fred King and the former director of the Atlanta Zoological Society, Gerard Hegstrom, and in several meetings over the next few years we reached a general agreement to build these large, natural ape environments to house Yerkes animals on loan to the zoo. In 1984, I made the Yerkes agreement one of my first priorities as director, and Bob Petty and Dr. King signed an agreement within the first few weeks of my administration. This move was a huge public relations success, increasing public confidence in the new zoo team, and it was the beginning of a solid, mutually beneficial relationship between the zoo and Yerkes. I was happy for the gorillas, too, knowing that they would benefit from the innovative exhibits we were planning. As for Willie B., his day in the sun was one step closer to reality.

By the end of 1985, we had updated the zoo's master

plan to accommodate these and other new ideas. Jon Coe and I, together with key zoo staff, then conspired to spend some time in the forests of Africa and Asia, where we learned all we could about the environment, from the lichens right up to the tree tops, taking photographs and sketching various spots for re-creation in the zoo. One of the greatest challenges was fitting our grand design for the apes into the existing space at the zoo. Our hilly topography was actually a great advantage to Coe, so he could create sight lines whereby people must look up to the animals. We knew we wanted to build at least three gorilla enclosures, surrounded by dry moats that would be hidden from the public's view by vegetation and rock work. I feared that the silverback males, motivated by competition, might jump into the moats to challenge their neighbors, so we decided to create double moats, which prevents gorillas from different troops from jumping into the same moat. (In practice, we had only a few gorillas enter the moats, and only in the first days of their exposure to the exhibits. So the moats seem to prevent fighting effectively.)

Our existing landscape was difficult to deal with, since we were committed to saving the large, hardwood trees in the area. This meant that in some areas the visitor would be surrounded by gorillas on only three sides, instead of all the way around. All in all, we decided to devote fully 10 percent of the zoo's entire acreage to the gorilla exhibit, a fairly bold commitment. By the time we were done we had moved more than 26,000 tons of soil and planted more than 3,500 trees and shrubs. We created special casings to protect the large hardwood trees, and created boulders and rock banks with steel frameworks and Gunite.

The big hardwoods were difficult to protect, since we had to safeguard root systems from all forms of intrusion, including the impact of heavy trucks and loads of construction materials. My staff had to work hard every day to keep the trees clear of debris and contact. Construction is messy by nature, and construction crews are not as sensitive to

African lions at Zoo Atlanta occupy an enclosure that resembles an African kopje, or rocky substrate. Here the animals appear to be in the African plains. (Photograph by Joe Sebo)

the needs of trees as they should be. Fortunately, a few months into construction, we hired a full-time horticulturist who patrolled the hardwoods as if they were his own. For my part, I constantly inquired about the state of our trees and beat my chest repeatedly in construction meetings. By our vigilance, we kept the zoo's botanical losses to a minimum and preserved some of its most beautiful specimens for future generations to enjoy.

Later, we applied our experiences traveling in east Africa to the task of designing our Masai Mara exhibit. Here we created a simulation of the African plains for antelope, giraffe, zebra, ostrich, and other birds to inhabit together, as they do in Kenya's Masai Mara Reserve. We built a separate habitat for lions, whose rocky outcropping (or *kopje*) is designed after those we saw in Africa, permitting these predators to gaze upon the antelope and other prey, just beyond their reach.

While simulations of this kind are key design elements in the modern zoo, we must not ignore the human beings who also occupy the zoo. We had to program the space for visitors, educators, and keepers, as well. For the keepers and veterinary staff, for example, we designed a state-of-the-art night holding building with an abundance of rooms for the gorillas. We created a series of overhead tunnels and fifty-seven hydraulic sliding doors, which meant that we could move gorillas around easily, as might be necessary for medical care and introductions of new animals.

For visitors (as well as the animals), we wanted to re-create the plant material of these tropical lands. But, since our climate can be challenging in winter, this was not an easy problem to solve. In 1987, we recruited Don Jackson, a talented horticulturist from the Cincinnati Zoo and Botanical Gardens, one of America's best landscaped zoos. Together with our design team, Jackson soon came up with some unique ideas for re-creating the botanical appearance of Africa and Indonesia for our newest exhibits. Honeylocust trees were chosen to simulate the distinctive acacia trees of the African savanna, and their lower branches were pruned to simulate foraging by giraffes. Even the Southern magnolia played a role, since it looks tropical and its leaves are shaped like those of the more tropical schefflera. In addition, some tropical plants, like banana trees, were used to adorn the exhibit areas during the warm seasons, then brought inside to greenhouses for the winter.

After traveling to the wild to study natural habitats, I became increasingly convinced that we could go beyond the simple display of animals in re-created environments. We could, perhaps, find a way to teach visitors about the lands these animals come from, such as who the native people are and what their culture is like. For example, I had noted while traveling in east Africa that the national parks provided many bilingual signs. I was fascinated by the Swahili phrases for "Beware of Lions," and "Elephants Have Right of Way," and thought about ways to render our zoo signage bilingual, so our zoo could be more "safari-like." Back in Atlanta, I assigned our resident expert in Swahili, John Fowler, to provide translations for us. We even built a sign that advises visitors to our African exhibits to "Enter at Your Own Risk," providing a bit of excitement, reinforced later when they cannot locate the barriers that keep the animals from escaping.

For additional realism, we scattered artifacts along public pathways for visitors to discover—a simulated termite mound here, an elephant skull there, some animal footprints elsewhere. Some of these artifacts have signage to explain them. Others are left for people to find and contemplate on their own. These are the types of discoveries one makes in the national parks of Africa, so it is a quite realistic experience. Volunteers and staff routinely identify the artifacts for visitors and discuss their significance.

In addition, we tried to pattern some of our building architecture after the tribal architecture of designated regions in Africa and Asia. For example, we built a 52-foot tribal hut near the zoo entrance, modeled after a genuine Cameroonian hut studied during one of our design expeditions. A shelter in the Indonesian section is built to resemble a tribal longhouse from Sumatra.

Finally, we tried to represent native cultures in activities and events throughout the zoo. To this end we depended on the knowledge of other experts. To the Ford African Rainforest we brought specialized dancers and musicians, storytellers and craftspeople. Kids appreciate tales about animals, and animals appear in the stories of all of the world's people. However, while tribal animal stories often illustrate the wisdom and wonder of animals, they rarely invoke conservation. For this reason, we hold competitions to create new stories, tales that tout conservation. In this way, we encourage the merging of our educational message with the cultural tradition of storytelling, and we show our visitors that animals do not live in isolation from humankind. Animals must contend with people, and people must contend with animals. The

This polar bear's grotto fits Sommer's definition of "hard" architecture. The grottoes will be demolished in 1994 to make room for the naturalistic Okefenokee Swamp. (Photograph by Terry L. Maple)

problem of coexistence, in fact, is at the heart of the story of conservation, and one that we address in greater detail through our more formal education programs.

The transformation of the life of Willie B. paralleled our creation of these new, multifaceted exhibits. His story is symbolic of our overall revolution. Since Willie B. had always lived a solitary life, we created a small island for him, but one that was located right in the middle of the other gorilla habitats. We didn't feel too bad about it, since "bachelor" gorilla males have been discovered in the wild. Our greatest worry was introducing Willie to his new, natural habitat, after twenty-seven years in a 20' x 40' indoor enclosure. We even hired an animal trainer to assist. But still, we feared he would be seriously disturbed by the changes, and we knew that some gorillas in other zoos had waited weeks before venturing into a new exhibit. Some of them never made the transition at all.

The process began several months before we planned to open the exhibits to the public, and before the other gorillas began to arrive from Yerkes. Willie B. was tranquilized and transferred by van to the night holding building. His longtime keeper, Charles Horton, stayed with him until he woke up, and on throughout the night, hoping to ease the gorilla's transition to this new building. Within a day or so, Willie was ready to explore his new surroundings, especially the small window that led to the outside. He also learned, with help from his keepers and trainer, to climb through overhead tunnels from cage to cage, and to move through small doors opening up into the different rooms of this still empty building.

Soon it was time for the big day—when he would be offered the chance to step outside for the first time. Charles Horton arrived early that morning, which happened to be a steamy warm Friday the 13th in May. He brought some of Willie's favorite fruits—watermelon, berries, and oranges. Key zoo staff and I had been positioned in adjacent moats to facilitate observation. Other zoo staff observed from down the hill, on the future visitor platform. Everyone was very quiet, partly to avoid alarming Willie, and partly because we were so apprehensive ourselves. We turned our two-way radios down low, and knelt in the tall wet grass to wait.

"Are we ready?" radioed general curator Dr. Dietrich Schaaf, when everything seemed to be in place. "Ready," answered Charles Horton, who was positioned in a special enclosure next to Willie B., along with mammal curator Sam Winslow and our visiting animal trainer, Tim Desmond.

"Door open," radioed Schaaf. There was silence, and the small door leading from Willie's room to the outdoors slid open by remote control. Willie put one foot out, then one arm, then pulled them back in. This went on for about twenty minutes, with Willie's eyes darting back and forth furtively. "He's going back and forth over the threshold," whispered Schaaf softly on his radio to those holding their breath down the hill. "Just what we would expect." Finally, the temptation was too much and he stepped all the way out. "It's just wonderful," I said into my wireless microphone, recording the emotion for posterity (and for television). "Willie is showing great courage. Now he's reaching up, grabbing a branch of the tree, pulling it. . . . This is a very special day for all of us." Just then the sky opened up and small raindrops began to fall. We waited silently for a reaction from Willie, knowing that gorillas are no great fans of water. When the rain finally penetrated his thick, graying fur, Willie arched his great back, let go of the branch, turned quickly and ran back inside. In spite of the rain, everyone at the zoo knew the morning had been a success. Willie B. had made the transition to outdoor life. Some of us were unable to contain our tears of joy.

That afternoon, the scene was replayed, with Willie B. emerging like a star for reporters and photographers of media from the *New York Times* to the Associated Press. We were national news again, but this time it was wonderful news. As word went out of Willie's big day, calls came in from radio stations as far away as Alaska and Toronto, all asking the same question: "Did he make it?" Loyal zoo supporters had already been calling the zoo for days to check on Willie B. Some even wrote letters directly to him. Volunteers who had weathered the bad times with the zoo now stood with pride. The next day, both local newspapers sported front-page pictures and stories, and soon we learned that papers across the country had carried notice of Willie. Our dream of seeing this symbolic, great animal freed had come true.

During the next few weeks, the gorillas from Yerkes began to arrive, and Willie had his first chance since infancy to see his own kind, and to watch as they were introduced to their own natural habitats. By mid-June, the entire exhibit was ready to open, and it drew the largest crowds of paying visitors the zoo had ever seen. Jon Coe and I wandered among the crowds looking for signs that

At last, Willie could venture outside for the first time in twenty-seven years! Here in the Ford African Rainforest, note his unusually large head, expressive face, and regal posture. (Photograph by Joe Sebo)

our exhibits were working for the people, too. Children immediately noticed a difference in Willie B. They cheered him, sang his praises, and noticed how magnificent he looked. Some folks thought he looked bigger, and everyone said he looked happier. He had been transformed from a felonious creature to a creature in harmony with nature. Happily, even in this state of nature, it seemed that Willie B. still liked people and continued to sit close to his adoring public. In those early days, we noticed some visitors weep with joy as they gazed upon him. They seemed to know that Willie, like the zoo itself, had been renewed, and that better days were ahead for all of us.

In many ways, our gorilla exhibits were even more successful than we could have hoped. We noticed breeding activity almost immediately and were celebrating the birth of three baby gorillas just nine months after the exhibit opened. (The first gorilla was born while I was traveling in east Africa. After a day in the bush, I was presented with a telex message congratulating me on the "birth of your first baby"! Simultaneous celebrations ensued in Atlanta and Kenya.) By spring of the next year, we were ready to take our experiment even one step further and begin the slow process of introducing Willie B. to female gorillas. First we put them in adjacent rooms during the night, separated only by some wire mesh. Then we allowed the females to join him. The older female, Katoomba, approached Willie with fists flying, but he was able to fend off her charge without causing harm. The younger female, Kinyani, took an immediate liking to Willie, and just two months later, they copulated for the first time. In mating he'd surprised us again, and we hoped that maybe we had helped by creating an environment in which he could observe normal gorilla socialization among the other troops. Recently, Willie was introduced to two additional females, and we hope that we will one day have the joy of welcoming his offspring to the world, since he has now mated with a female who has been a successful mother.

We had equal success with the opening of our orangutan exhibits just a few months after the opening of the Ford African Rainforest. Orangutans who had never seen a tree took quickly to our tall climbing structures and can now be seen from throughout the zoo. Visitors run to get closer, and when they arrive at the overlook, they crane their necks upward and gawk in wonder. Now we can fully appreciate the agility of these creatures, whose essential character requires an arboreal lifestyle. Of course, in the wild orangutans occasionally drop debris onto human observers. If I could arrange for a safe way for this to happen in our exhibits, I would add this bit of reality as well.

Now, several years later, we can say, with pride, that our exhibit ideas have been successful in providing better environments for both zoo animals and visitors. Our animals exhibit natural behaviors and most are breeding successfully. Two of our exhibits have been honored with national awards for excellence. Our visitors are happy with the dense, green landscaping and thrilled when they see young gorillas playing in the forest, or large, hairy orangutans swinging by an arm from a tree branch fifty feet above the ground. No one laughs, sneers, or holds their nose when they look at our monkeys, apes, and large cats. Instead, they sometimes stand with their mouths open, enthralled at the sight of a 400-pound gorilla sitting next to the bush just a few feet away.

ON THE CARE AND FEEDING OF A CAUSE

The zoo is a weird, wonderful, exciting, frustrating, glorious, rewarding, disheartening, beautiful place to work.
Theodore H. "Ted" Reed, Director Emeritus, National Zoo

I became director of the Atlanta Zoo in a crisis, during which I was suddenly challenged by every obscure facet of zoo management. There was no public relations department, no marketing plan or personnel, and a dysfunctional management system. The zoo was isolated in its misery, since no other organizations wanted to be associated with it. So, in addition to dealing with the formidable animal and exhibit problems, I had to formulate speedy plans to improve the zoo's image, promote it to the public and its potential supporters, and motivate the staff to function smoothly and effectively. It was a challenge worthy of a career diplomat.

When I was seventeen, I had hoped to pursue a career in the foreign service, using this platform as a way to help solve some of the world's problems but without the phoniness of traditional politics. As president of the student body, I was politically active in high school and had always been a leader among my peers. After I entered college, and changed my major to psychology, I didn't realize that these same leanings would continue to loom large in my life. But when I landed in the middle of the Atlanta Zoo crisis, these latent skills came in handy.

First, I had to establish myself as a person who could get things done, and get them done quickly. Time was of the essence in June 1984; I had to win the confidence of the public, the city, and the staff as quickly as possible. This opportunity might never come again, I reasoned. Luckily, I was able to negotiate a direct reporting relationship to Carolyn Hatcher, the city commissioner who handled the zoo, hire an experienced administrative assistant who knew the inner workings of city government, and bring a swift (albeit temporary) resolution to the veterinary crisis. With these tasks accomplished, I was able to address the long list of immediate improvements that the USDA, AAZPA, and city inspectors required.

To stifle the stream of negative publicity, the city had formulated a "gag rule" whereby only designated staff were permitted to talk to the press. But I didn't enforce it. No chief executive appreciates "leaks," and I was no exception, but I had to sympathize with the staff who had long labored in a failed system of management. After all, their revolutionary zeal was not that different from mine, and the leaks had done their job; the zoo now had a revolutionary director. I could hardly punish them for something that needed to be done. If I had been a zookeeper in 1984, I would have been on the side of the leakers.

Once I had assumed my duties as zoo director, the leaks continued a while. The leakers were still skeptical. On one occasion, staff belonging to the AFSCME union called a press conference just outside my office door, and failed to tell me about it. But these were only symptoms of much larger problems. I elected to ignore symptoms, as the team concentrated on bigger problems that needed our full attention. As the new leaders proved themselves, scandalous material became harder to find. One incident helped to turn the situation around. While I was in Miami at the national AAZPA conference, a reptile keeper back in Atlanta experienced an accident and a rare Indian crocodile was injured. It wasn't a result of mismanagement or incompetence, it was just an accident. Someone—apparently the target of previous leaks—leaked the incident to the press. This, after all, was a time when the zoo staff was still distinctly polarized. Once more, like vultures on the Serengeti Plains, a flock of investigative reporters descended upon the zoo. It was a painful lesson, and I couldn't resist the opportunity to preach: "Live by the sword, die by the sword." On that day in September 1984, the leaks abruptly ended. The keepers who first blew the whistles are still working at the zoo.

As director, I felt my direct reporting relationship to Commissioner Hatcher was crucial since it elevated the zoo to a position of equality among Parks, Recreation and Cultural Affairs. The zoo had to be front burner, and I was afraid that it would drift back to mediocrity if the zoo director could be stopped by an intermediary. But the commissioner was totally committed to fixing the zoo, so this was an easy decision for her.

I had to have a savvy administrative assistant who could find a path through the maze of bureaucratic impediments. In fact, my ignorance of city government was a major disadvantage. Early in our working relationship, I proclaimed to Susan Hood, "I don't know a thing about city government, and I don't ever want to know anything about it." I didn't want to become part of the bureaucratic entanglements that had plagued the zoo for so long. Instead, I intended to be a problem solver. I could spot a problem with ease, and in most cases the solution was simple, but I needed an experienced manager to find a way to get things done.

One of my first problems on the job was finding a replacement for the vacant assistant curator position. We needed high-quality middle management, and I had located a talented candidate among the staff at the Riverbanks Zoo. His name was John Croxton. However, while I needed Croxton right away, city regulations required that sufficient time pass equal to the previous curator's unused sick and

U.S. Representative Newt Gingrich inspects Coca the elephant in 1985.
(Photograph courtesy of Conway—Atlanta, Photography)

vacation time before I could hire a replacement. Since the retired curator had accumulated several centuries of leave time, I would be retired myself before I could replace him! This was a really inane problem. To transform the zoo, I needed to hire a bright young curator immediately. Susan Hood found the way. It was called "the emergency provision." All I had to do was obtain a declaration of emergency in order to circumvent the rules. The mayor's office capitulated, and I had my curator. We had to bend a lot of rules to fix the zoo, but we were able to do a lot in the one year and one month during which I ran the zoo as a department of city government. Susan Hood and John Croxton were the foot soldiers who fought hard in the trenches during that tough first year.

One of my best decisions as zoo director has been to hire Dr. Rita McManamon, but I was simply the one who recruited her. There would have been no position to fill if Commissioner Hatcher had not found a way to hire a new veterinarian. When Dr. Emmett Ashley announced his leave of absence, the zoo could then alter its course of veterinary medicine. Dr. Ashley had been a contract, or part-time, veterinarian, but I elected to recruit a full-time collaborator who would be involved in both medicine and management. Carolyn Hatcher's resolute action enabled me to hire Dr. McManamon, who in turn created a first-class medical program for the zoo. Strong leadership; swift action; recruitment of talent; high standards; change; excellence—this is the way that longstanding problems get solved in the zoo, or anywhere else.

To face the animal situation rationally, it was necessary to hire many new staff members. Some of the existing zoo workers were simply out of synchrony with our goals and objectives. Changing staff is perhaps the most difficult thing a leader must do, but the Atlanta Zoo got better when we added additional qualified staff to deal with its problems. I attempted to recruit new staff exclusively from well-run, winning institutions (see the table on the next page). As soon

KEY STAFF RECRUITED TO ZOO ATLANTA AND THEIR ZOO PEDIGREE

Name/Position	Date Arrived	Previous Zoo
Rita McManamon *Veterinarian*	1984	San Francisco Zoo
Dietrich Schaaf *General Curator*	1984	Philadelphia Zoo
John Croxton *Curator of Mammals*	1984	Riverbanks Zoo
Guy Farnell *Curator of Birds*	1985	Audubon Zoo
Don Jackson *Curator of Horticulture*	1986	Cincinnati Zoo
Tony Vecchio *Curator of Mammals*	1986*	Riverbanks Zoo
John Fowler *Curator of Birds*	1986**	Audubon Zoo
Richard Block *Curator of Education*	1986	Kansas City Zoo
Sam Winslow *Curator of Mammals*	1988***	Audubon Zoo
Jeff Swanagan *Curator of Education*	1988****	Columbus Zoo
Gail Bruner *Zoo Biologist*	1989	Los Angeles Zoo
Deborah Forthman *Research*	1989	Los Angeles Zoo
Elizabeth Stevens *Research*	1990	National Zoo

*Replaced Croxton **Replaced Farnell ***Replaced Vecchio ****Replaced Block

as new leadership was firmly in place, so that we were working effectively on the many short-term problems, we focused on a long-term plan for the future, establishing a vision for our community and the new zoo team. With the help of our superb architecture and development consultants, we developed a surplus of innovative ideas with which to build the world-class exhibits we'd dreamed about.

One of the unsung sources of heroism in the Atlanta zoo story is the AAZPA accreditation process. AAZPA's scathing criticism of the zoo, and its action withdrawing the zoo's credentials of membership, was an ever-present "hammer" that drove our commitment to excellence. The three inspectors—Palmer "Satch" Kranz (Riverbanks Zoo, South Carolina), Wilbur Amand (Philadelphia), and George Felton (Baton Rouge, La.) left us a long list of priorities, and we steadily worked to correct these deficiencies during the first three years of my administration. The accreditation process also provided some direction for our master planning, as we attempted to remedy old problems while drafting a vision of our future.

The revised master plan developed by Coe & Lee Associates worked remarkably well wherever we unveiled it. The document built upon some excellent architecture produced by our local firms of Robert & Company and Turner Associates. When the three firms united, the product really came to life. No zoo director can properly articulate a zoo vision without excellent graphic representations of the future zoo. Coe & Lee (now CLRR, the world's leading zoo design firm) worked their magic in Atlanta because of the generosity of the Cecil B. Day family, who agreed to fund the plan. This was a historic vote of confidence for the zoo and a major turning point. Their participation was also a confidence builder for me, since I had traveled to Africa with many members and friends of the Day family in March 1985. Our vision of the zoo was based on the wilds of Africa and other places. As we toured together, we all talked about how to recapture the experience of communing with wildlife. Could a zoo ever be as grand as nature? Could we actually create a meaningful snapshot of Africa in Atlanta? The Day family, especially Kathie Day Gunther, who served two terms on our zoo board, helped me to envision a natural habitat zoo, and their confidence in me emboldened the plan itself. With the revised master plan in hand, selling the dream would be a slam dunk. Our community was about to be introduced to a world-class "futurezoo."

As we worked together to build this new zoo, I gradually developed my own leadership style. Since I had no formal management training, it was based on a combination of practical experience, longstanding beliefs, and a few ideas borrowed from sage philosophers and role models I had come to admire.

The most important component of my personal philosophy is *teamwork*. I knew from the very beginning that I could not solve the problems of this long-neglected zoo without a great deal of help. I was comfortable delegating tasks to my staff, once I had assembled a qualified group of senior managers. In addition to delegating important responsibilities, I tried to foster teamwork by making the zoo a nurturing place where cooperation and helpfulness were rewarded. For this approach, I am indebted to my former department chairman at Georgia Tech, Ed Loveland, who always made his professors feel good about coming to work. I tried to do as he did, by solving bureaucratic problems that might be holding back my staff, providing adequate resources, and buffering them from politics whenever possible. Periodically, I would invite my team to join me for a beer after work, and as word of this ritual circulated, the number of participants began to grow. Some people who had been having trouble adjusting to the new administrative direction found it easier to communicate under these conditions. In many cases, breakthrough discussions occurred and led to improved working relationships. As we lunched together and worked late together, we also laughed together and sometimes cried together. We became true colleagues, and zoo morale increased significantly in these early days.

We were also having a good time together, in spite of the huge challenge, and this encouraged me to promote another simple principle—think positively. I characterized my approach as "the management of joy," based on a phrase from the 1968 presidential campaign of Hubert H. Humphrey, whose exuberant style had been labeled the "politics of joy." I knew, even in the earliest days, that the zoo could be great, but the everyday frustrations were enormous. There were many days when I just wanted to quit, and then some small but significant victory would occur, or one of my hard-working staff would offer some uplifting counsel. So, I tried to combine positive thinking with good humor and fellowship, to make these painful problems bearable.

Of course, being in the zoo gave us all a unique advantage. When times got really tough, we could always commune or confer with the animals! There's nothing that makes you feel better faster than an audience of wild creatures, and nothing that revs up your spirits like the determination to improve their well-being. I have always felt that I was working on their behalf, and I continue to gain encouragement in their presence. Like many of the visitors

Professional soccer star Pelé dribbles with Starlet the elephant in a 1986 match arranged by the Ford Motor Company. (Photograph by Joe Sebo)

to the zoo in those days, I felt sorry for the animals in their terribly confined environments. Yet even behind bars, and in isolation from the world, they never lost their dignity. Somehow, that suggested to me that if we changed their conditions at our zoo, we would change a significant piece of the world.

Thinking a problem through carefully is equally important. In those tough, early days, when I needed to closely examine a sensitive issue or conflict, or figure out a creative solution to a stressful situation, I retreated to my "ivory tower" at Georgia Tech and tried to approach the problem rationally, in the manner of a scientist. From these moments I learned that quiet, reflective time is necessary for any administrator or leader. The day-to-day pressures can make it very difficult to think clearly, and problems begin to run together in a stream of chaos. Soon, the office seems to be out of control. By breaking away for a bit, one can reestablish a sense of control and come back with a fresh perspective, new ideas, or simply an adjusted attitude. So, I believe zoos (or any other "zoo-like" business) should contain some places where quiet time and contemplation are permitted, even encouraged. A reading room or library can be set up for this purpose. But it must be a place free from telephone interruptions. (McDonald's corporate headquarters, for example, has a womb-like meditation room.) I also believe in sabbaticals; these can benefit not just the leave-taker but the life of the institution itself. Unfortunately, the corporate world hasn't embraced this little idea from academe to any significant extent, but I think it could easily be adopted by the zoo world. In my graduate days, I was a Rotary Fellow; in the next few years I am hoping to qualify for a Fulbright Fellowship.

But improving the staff, morale, and atmosphere within the zoo was just part of the leadership challenge. No zoo, nor any other business, can function properly without constantly keeping its customers in mind, and this looms large in our management philosophy. In fact, from the very beginning, we knew that our visitors would expect elephants at the zoo, so I began planning an elephant exhibit for 1985. Those of us who were close to the action in 1984 have always felt indebted to Twinkles, the elephant who tragically died in a circus. Elephants may be the most charismatic of all the megavertebrates, so an offense against elephants generates a fair amount of anger and arousal. Atlanta's citizens were outraged at Twinkle's treatment, and this event must be regarded as the first genuine turning point in the Atlanta Zoo story.

Since we intended to feature Africa in much of the new exhibitry, it seemed reasonable to shop for some African elephants to inhabit the new zoo. I discovered that there were many orphaned elephants available due to the South African practice of "culling," whereby whole herds were killed to control the growth of elephant populations. Often, the babies were captured rather than killed and sold abroad to zoos and circuses. We acquired our first African elephant in just this way. We learned about a baby African from a dealer in Florida who was willing to sell the animal for one-fifth the price of an Asian elephant. With training, board, and transportation, the whole transaction would come to about $20,000.

After I received photographs of her, I contacted one of our most committed benefactors, Jay Crouse, who agreed to finance the purchase. Jay and I traveled to Baton Rouge, along with my children, Molly and Emily (then five and three years old respectively), to examine the first African elephant in our zoo's long history. She was just two and one-half years old, covered with a sparse coat of long, wiry hair, and equipped with a mischievous and wildly active trunk. She shared her compound with a little male. I think Jay would have purchased them both if I had asked him, but we knew that the male would grow to an intractable size and temperament, so—on behalf of Atlanta's children—we happily accepted the world's cutest baby elephant. The animal trainer lifted my children onto the backs of the two elephants, and they got the rides of their young lives. What a hoot that they rode elephants long before ever straddling a horse!

The zoo's nadir was marked by the mysterious death of an elderly elephant, but its renaissance would be illuminated by the arrival of Starlet O'Hara, a tiny baby elephant who, in 1987, would be featured in *USA Today* as one of the most famous zoo animals in America. Today Zoo Atlanta's three African elephants live well in their spacious naturalistic enclosure, a fitting monument to the many elephants—Coca, Cola, Delicious, Refreshing, Maude (to name a few)—who have delighted Atlanta's children for more than a century. Starlet and other new baby elephants were centerpieces for the new zoo and a major draw during the attendance surge of the 1980s.

Indeed, it has always been important for us to stay in close touch with our visitors. When I first came to the zoo, our potential customers were very disillusioned, so it was especially important to assess their needs. The best way to do this is to walk through the zoo every day. I can't cover the whole place on one walk, so I focus on a different piece each time. This may sound odd, since, after all, I work at the zoo. But, as in all businesses, it is just too easy to find oneself trapped in meetings all day long, whether at the office or in the community. So, I try to walk around the zoo as much as possible, and encourage other unit managers to do the same. Management consultants refer to this strategy as "management by walking around," and it really works. When you are in the position of the customer, you know whether your product is really working as it should. In the case of the zoo, it is also fun to stop and commune with the creatures, which are our noble raison d'être.

One of the best techniques I have for "managing by walking around" is to bring my family to the zoo. As they experience the zoo, they always make known to me any warts that may be showing. My wife is particularly skilled at finding fault with rest rooms, for example. It's amazing how a visit to the zoo, or any other public facility, can be spoiled by dirty rest rooms. So, whenever we encounter a dirty facility, we let it be known. Fortunately, my staff is even tougher than I am, and we have some of the cleanest rest rooms of any zoo anywhere. I check them, supervisors check them, maintenance workers sign off on them, and sometimes we deploy "secret shoppers" who double-check our vigilance. Another relevant experience I had with my family occurred near the reptile house, where my wife waited outside with several visitors who feared snakes. She noticed that there were no benches for those who waited, faintheartedly, outside the building. We added seating the very next weekend.

Hediger recognized that modern zoos are too large for the director to supervise all of the details of the operational system. However, he still regarded the director's "inspection" as the key to good zoo management:

> The word "inspection" comes from the Latin verb *inspicere*, meaning to look into. The morning inspection of the director—referred to almost everywhere as a thing of the past—consists of a looking-into and an active examination of all cages, dens, and enclosures; it includes the inspection of all spaces and corners of the establishment. . . . The paramount objective of the zoo inspection is to examine the results of the unique confrontation between man and animal, as presented by conditions in a zoo.

I have learned something else in my interactions with the public. No person should ever leave the zoo without a peak, personal experience, a unique insight, a new idea, or some unusual memento. People multiply these transactions many times over as they recollect and recite the details of their zoo visit. To do this right, we must be prepared to provide our supporters, partners, and guests with specialized bumper stickers, pins, T-shirts, ties, and coffee mugs. The successful zoo must be carefully and constantly marketed to its public. In my own life, I've come to realize that I must always be "zooey." I drive a zooey Ford Explorer, wear zooey shirts and ties (I own nearly 100), sport wildlife pins and pendants, and cover my head with a solar-powered pith helmet.

Another way we try to maintain contact with our public

Orangutans climb to fifty-five feet in Zoo Atlanta's new exhibit.
(Photograph courtesy of the *Chattanooga Times*)

is by soliciting and responding to feedback. Much of it comes to us unsolicited, through personal contact, letters, and phone calls, and we pay close attention to it. As a result, we know what we're doing well, and where we need to improve. We make it a priority to address any issue our public brings to our attention. Sometimes people are critical, but more often, I have found, they are kind. Once I was approached by a little boy who couldn't have been more than four years old. His smiling father was waving him on, urging him to approach me. I bent down to say "hi" and he whispered to me, in a meek little monotone: "Thank you; thank you for the zoo." The sincerity of that compliment brought tears to my eyes. It still does.

We have also benefitted in this regard from pro bono assistance provided by one of Atlanta's most talented marketing researchers. For seven years, Ken Hollander and his associates have conducted an annual "visitor exit survey" for the zoo's marketing committee. The survey investigates visitor attitudes and behavior and provides information about problems and opportunities that our staff can then address. In 1992 the survey addressed visitation patterns, purchasing activity, waiting times, distances traveled to reach the zoo, member status, satisfaction with the zoo, satisfaction with the food and drink, perceived value, reasons for visiting the zoo, coupon usage, and other marketing issues. For example, the survey asked visitors questions such as, "How many times have you visited the zoo this year?" and "How would you rate today's visit on a scale of 1 to 10?"

The Hollander survey has proved to be a useful planning tool. For example, the survey identified serious problems in food service in 1991, so we made many adjustments in preparation for the next year. The 1992 survey indicated that these changes were succeeding, as visitor satisfaction with food and service increased dramatically. Furthermore, the percentage of visitors who reported food and drink purchases had a significant increase.

To be successful with families, our zoo must always be clean, friendly, and high in quality. The entire staff takes pride in the visitor satisfaction data, which have risen steadily during the last five years. In 1988, Hollander reported a 7.3 satisfaction rating (out of 10), followed by 7.5, 8.1, 8.2, and 8.4 in the following years. As good as these scores may be, our fastidious managers will not be satisfied with anything less than perfection. Every zoo should conduct visitor exit surveys on a regular basis and subject the data to skilled interpretation by experts like Ken Hollander. This is a wonderful example of how our community is helping us hone our skills and improve our product.

Last, but not least, since the beginning we have observed the giants of our industry and try to learn from them. There are many potential role models, since everybody does something better than somebody else. So, we try to keep in close contact with other attractions, aquariums, museums, and zoos, and we learn from each other. In terms of what we at Zoo Atlanta can do, as a reasonably small zoo, I have always regarded Chicago's Lincoln Park Zoo as our most appropriate model. At 35 acres, Lincoln Park is slightly smaller than we are (37.5 acres), yet it has a much larger collection, an excellent reputation, a tremendous fund-raising organization, and huge numbers of visitors. (It is also one of the last free zoos.) It also has many programs that we would do well to emulate. On the other hand, we are certainly the equal of Lincoln Park in terms of our science and education programs, which makes me think we really are headed toward the top of the zoo profession.

The San Diego Zoo also has some wonderful things for us to imitate. It is the best in the zoo world at making its services friendly and a good experience for the public, from clean facilities to high-quality gift and food shops. Whenever we address our own food and gift operations, I think of San Diego. San Diego is also a leader in publicizing and marketing its zoo, and I like to think we are moving in a similar direction. When it comes to horticulture, San Diego also leads, so I was very pleased when some of their staff recently came to study our gorilla facilities for help in designing their own new exhibit.

Sometimes imitation provides other lessons as well. The San Diego Zoo has a huge, diverse collection of animals, and people can see a great variety in one place. But a huge collection has its down side. It's not possible to give every animal a wonderful living experience when you have so many and such variety. In general, zoos can do better if they devote themselves to creating the best facilities for fewer species, and that is what we have tried to do in Atlanta. San Diego is now rapidly trying to emulate the wonderful natural habitat exhibits that smaller, more specialized zoos have built, which is one reason they elected to study our gorilla facilities. In recent years, they have built award-winning exhibits for tigers and gorillas, and they broke new ground with their innovative "Wild Animal Park" in the early 1970s.

But San Diego's immense animal collection is always impressive. On a recent visit there, I had good reason to inspect their large group of huge Galapagos tortoises (males can weigh up to 400 pounds!). In the early 1970s, our reptile staff sent two tortoises to San Diego to assist with their breeding program. Our people believed that the animals were females, but they turned out to be males (sexing tortoises was not a simple task in those days). I met the two animals up close and personal, and they are awesome creatures. It brought back memories of the days when San Diego children were permitted to ride them! On this visit, I vowed to help "downsize" the collection of my good friends in San Diego, by reclaiming these tortoises for exhibition in Atlanta. Given the size of their group, San Diego won't miss two adult males. For our part, we intend to acquire females and exhibit the group alongside our giant Aldabra tortoises. I am confident that this acquisition will delight all Atlantans, especially the children who are so fascinated by the size of these gentle giants.

Zoo professionals actually participate in conservation in three ways: ex situ, in situ, and conservation education. The best-known form of zoo conservation is captive propagation, or "ex situ" conservation. Many of the species that we successfully breed in the zoo are rare and endangered species. Many of these are carefully managed by Species Survival Plan (SSP) committees organized by AAZPA. Throughout the world, zoos are organizing to form regional management units based on the SSP model. For example, European zoos work together through management committees of their equivalent of SSP, whose offices are based at the Artis Zoo in Amsterdam.

The commitment of zoos to "in situ" conservation is more recent and less publicized. Not willing to be "the last refuge" (read "last resting place"!) for endangered species, zoos have become increasingly involved in conservation projects around the world. For example, Zoo Atlanta takes pride in its work to save elephants and gorillas in Rwanda, drill baboons on the west African island of Bioko, crocodiles and other fauna in Belize, and orangutans in Indonesia. We will become even more involved in Africa when our field fellowship program begins in June 1993. By supporting the work of wildlife biologist Dr. Tom Butynski, we will be active in developing national parks and reserves in east, central, and west African countries.

The best examples of field conservation by a single zoo organization is the extraordinary work of the New York Zoological Society, but there are other American zoos that routinely contribute financial and human resources to field conservation. These include the Audubon Zoo in New Orleans, Brookfield and Lincoln Park zoos (Chicago), the Cincinnati Zoo, the Los Angeles Zoo, the National Zoo, the Milwaukee Zoo, Miami Metrozoo, the Minnesota Zoo, Omaha's Henry Doorly Zoo, the Phoenix Zoo, the San Francisco Zoo, the San Diego Zoo, the St. Louis Zoo, and Seattle's Woodland Park Zoo, to name a

WSB-TV anchorwoman Chris Curle interacts with Galapagos tortoises during the taping of Zoo Atlanta's expedition to the Galapagos Islands. Zoo Atlanta soon will open a new exhibit for giant tortoises.
(Photograph by Terry L. Maple)

few. It is encouraging that the list of participants is growing by leaps and bounds.

Of course the conservation awareness campaigns that virtually all good zoos practice do not require large expenditures of money or people. Still, we must improve the reach and strength of our conservation message, since so much of the earth is in peril. By strengthening zoos and nature centers in the developing world, we can make more education outreach programs possible. The mere presence of conservation-minded professionals can deter poachers and interlopers who, by their irresponsible action, would destroy irreplaceable wildlife habitat.

Zoo conservation encompasses all of the science- and education-based projects and programs that contribute to wildlife conservation in the field or in the zoo itself. The larger zoos generally contribute in all of the possible ways, but even small zoos can play a role as members of an outreach consortium, such as the Madagascar Fauna Group

(MFG) or the Zoo Conservation Outreach Group (Zoo COG), each of which is doing important work in African and South American countries that harbor highly endangered wildlife. It is important to recognize that zoo professionals are working to save not only animals but also the habitats that support them.

Management is a subject one never finishes learning about. I realized when I became director that it would take years for me to master the management literature, so I've also tried to acquire additional training through short courses and seminars and by listening to more experienced managers. However, I did not accept the directorship thinking that it would be merely an exercise in management. The zoo certainly needed good management, but its most urgent need was for *strong leadership*. In their book *Leaders* (1985), Warren Bennis and Burt Nanus suggest that a manager "does things right," while a leader "does the right things." That seemed to be a good distinction in my case. The zoo had hundreds of problems to be solved in 1984, but I was confident that I could find the answers and ultimately change the zoo with strong leadership, diligence, and teamwork.

As I was learning to manage the zoo, the foundations of our marketing and promotions philosophy emerged as well. Because of the zoo's many problems and our severely tarnished public image, two attributes had to be emphasized: credibility and a solid code of animal management ethics. If the community didn't believe in us, they would never support us, nor would they visit us. We'd be out of business. But this credibility could only be based on the work we were actually doing and the staff who were doing it. Therefore, the work and the staff had to be of exemplary quality.

I saw this clearly on my very first day as director of the zoo, when I telephoned Bob Wagner, then executive director of the American Association of Zoological Parks and Aquariums. I had set returning the zoo to membership in AAZPA as my first big goal, and I wanted Wagner to know that I was committed to turning the zoo around. As we discussed the situation, I detected anger in his voice. I knew he was speaking for the entire zoo world when he told me that the Atlanta zoo would have to do much more than meet the standards of AAZPA if it wanted to pass the accreditation inspection. Reading between the lines, I could see that we would be scrutinized like no other zoo in the history of AAZPA's accreditation program.

So, to build up our chances, and our credibility, we decided to adopt very tough standards of animal management for our zoo. If we did not have the proper space for an animal, we would move it, and only to the most reputable institution. We also decided that we would not use euthanasia as a management tool for unwanted or old animals, as some zoos did. If we could not find a good institution for an animal that did not fit into our new exhibit plans, we would make a place for it somewhere else in the zoo. Such animals have served the public well and deserve a comfortable life, we reasoned. We also have provided animals that were too old or infirm to live with others with a comfortable place to retire. Our old male lion Valentino was a case in point. Since he had only one eye, we were afraid that if we put him in our new exhibit with younger, female lions, he might be injured. So, we retired him to a renovated, outdoor enclosure in the off-exhibit part of the zoo. He lived out the rest of his life in reasonable comfort. We also decided to allow old animals to continue on exhibit if their health permitted it. The gorilla Massa of the Philadelphia Zoo is a fair illustration of this standard. He was on exhibit until he reached the incredibly ripe old gorilla age of fifty-four. Although he was thin, completely gray, and nearly toothless, Massa remained a visitor favorite until the end.

With credibility and ethics as our foundation, we then

had to consider the two basic ways to market a zoo: marketing it as a cause (now known as social marketing, with the aim of changing attitudes and behaviors) and marketing it as any other competitive business. We decided to do it both ways. Devoting ourselves to conservation and education helped us attract the attention of socially conscious benefactors and foundations and also helped to demonstrate our credibility. I've found that it is relatively easy to raise money for the zoo once I've had the opportunity to describe fully the scope of our education and conservation programs, and the many ways we are trying to save the earth's wildlife. Even the skeptical are usually won over when I add presentations by key staff members, in-depth expertly written proposals for funds, or lists of our successful programs and scientific publications. Zoo Atlanta's superb staff are the best "sales people" in the zoo world.

Of course, in order to attract as many visitors and as much support to the zoo as possible, we also had to market

The modern zoo must provide close but safe encounters for its millions of visitors, such as these children on a behind-the-scenes tour at Tampa's Busch Gardens. (Photograph by Terry L. Maple)

the zoo as a business. In this regard, we adopted some of the techniques and methods commonly used by entertainment and amusement enterprises, such as Disney World and Six Flags. We printed T-shirts and bumper stickers, created wild billboards, and ran ads in the newspaper promoting special events that we developed for the public. Of course, since we're a nonprofit organization without a large marketing budget, we often have to obtain donated advertising space, or get it at some special rate. Our marketing was aimed at drawing visitors and benefactors to the zoo, but we were also marketing our dream of a great, "new" Atlanta Zoo. Every time we had something specific to promote, we also attached our message for the future, our dream of becoming the "world's next great zoo."

I began to see that being creative, and even funny at times, could go a long way in promoting our cause. When I was a full-time college professor, I sometimes felt that I had to constrain my creativity in order to be more objective and scientific. Yet, sometimes I couldn't resist. In 1975 I observed crows dropping walnuts on hard surfaces, noticing that they often dropped them on highways, where cars would come along and crush the nuts. I concluded from this that the crows had, in effect, "intelligently" dropped nuts in locations where they were likely to be broken. When I collected these notes for publication, I conjured up the title "Do Crows Use Automobiles as Nutcrackers?" and published the piece in the journal *Western Birds*. Now, whenever someone looks over the publication list on my vita, they usually turn to me and ask: "*Do* crows use automobiles as nutcrackers?" Far from hurting me, the unusual title actually has called attention to my work. Years later, the prestigious bird journal *Condor* published a paper entitled "Crows *Do* Use Automobiles as Nutcrackers," in which they confirmed my observations. I learned just how far creativity could take me, although I knew that my title succeeded only because it was based on careful observations. You can't be creative or funny unless you are credible.

Hediger gave a similar warning against making false claims in his book *Man and Animal in the Zoo* (1969) in a discussion about a new zoo diet:

> There is no doubt that every zoo should take pride in its work; public relations, propaganda and advertisement all have an important place in the management of a zoo, but the work done by these departments should not become mixed up with that of zoo biology if the advantages of scientific feeding methods are to be assessed seriously.

A few months after the Ford African Rainforest opened, and after Willie B. was on exhibit with his new harem (but before he started breeding), we decided to have some fun, even though we were very serious about the primary business of exhibiting, breeding, and studying gorillas. One of Atlanta's most esteemed public relations experts, Virgil Shutze, suggested a campaign based on the question of whether Willie B. would ever become a successful breeder. His firm created two huge billboards, depicting two gorillas and the burning question: "Will he or won't he?" As if on cue, just a few weeks after the billboards appeared, Willie started breeding for the first time. The media went wild with the news, which was broadcast on the radio just a few hours after the breeding was discovered, and followed by front-page stories in all the newspapers. Actually, a variation of the "will he or won't he" theme had been suggested to me back in 1986, by Ford marketing executive Jim Donaldson, who asked, "Willie B. a lover or a fighter?" But the zoo's reputation was so shaky then that I lacked the confidence to take a chance with our image and promote this phrase. By 1989 our credibility was soaring, so I decided to accept the billboards. They were a smashing success.

Many zoos have become quite sophisticated at marketing themselves, often working with public relations and marketing agencies. These professionals have helped zoos compete by directing advertising, exhibit openings, special events, and other programs. At Zoo Atlanta, for example, our agency partners have helped us promote new animals, unusual animal births, special exhibits, and advertising and fund-raising campaigns. Not unexpectedly, zoos have begun to use all sorts of clever promotions and slogans. For instance, the San Francisco Zoo was successful with its campaign to free the gorillas ("The gorillas are loose"), which they used when creating new naturalistic exhibits. Similarly, the Cleveland Zoo successfully marketed a new warthog exhibit by promoting the animal as "the ugliest creature on earth." This campaign did not distort the image of the warthog or portray it inaccurately, since this animal has a squat body sparsely covered with wiry black hairs and protruding "wartlike" knobs covering its head. Its sheer ugliness attracts many visitors to the zoo. In a print advertisement produced for Zoo Atlanta by local advertising firm BBDO/South, a closeup of our gorilla Willie B. was introduced by a bold headline proclaiming: "Please give generously. He has a wife and 186,234 children to educate." Published in *Fortune* and other magazines, the ad went on to explain how the zoo was reaching out to the children in our community so that they might learn about the world's endangered wildlife. This clever message was well received in our community.

In addition to developing creative tactics and using professional expertise, one of the real keys to the success of our marketing efforts has been the formation of partnerships, with benefactors, businesses, celebrities, and media. With such partners at our sides, we have been able to accomplish some incredible things. One of our earliest, and most important, partners turned out to be the Ford Motor Company. In 1986, when we were just at the beginning of our redevelopment, I was contacted by a local public relations expert, Jan Pringle, of the Pringle Dixon Pringle agency. Jan is a big supporter of the zoo and had learned of a large company that was looking to link with a cause in our community. Without identifying the company by name, she asked me to develop a list of about ten ideas for working with this potential corporate partner. We had plenty of ideas. The most compelling was our plan to visit Africa to study the habitats of wild gorillas, in order to apply this knowledge to the building of our new exhibits. Jan suggested that we invite some members of the local media to join us on the expedition so that the public could learn about our activities. This resulted in our historic agreement with WSB, the local ABC affiliate, to develop a prime-time television special about gorillas. Our corporate partner came on board and agreed to underwrite the costs of the expedition, the television production, and the advertising. This was just the beginning of a long and fruitful partnership with both the Ford Motor Company and WSB, and we have since made four one-hour television specials together. (Ford also sponsors our new gorilla habitats and our black-tie gala, the Beastly Feast.) We have also made special programs with other stations, including our public television station, GPTV. Our programs have performed well in the ratings and have won six local Emmy awards. We feel that these shows have played a major role in bringing the public closer to our mission at the zoo, and in encouraging people to support and visit us.

Through our television partnerships, we also brought a number of celebrities on board to promote the zoo. Television personality Virginia Gunn hosted our first show, and actress Stephanie Powers joined us for our second program, taped in Indonesia. WSB anchor Chris Curle participated in all but the first special, and she has labored long on our behalf. Her dedication to the cause is so great that she agreed to join our board of directors.

Our unique position in the community has also given us the opportunity to partner with a variety of public figures, such as politicians, entrepreneurs, media moguls, and others. Often these partnerships emerge from behind-the-scenes tours that we offer community leaders who seem to have an interest in animals. I can still remember the first tour I provided for our Republican congressman Newt Gingrich, back in 1985. I was just starting my second year as director when Newt requested a tour. Congressman Gingrich is an outspoken and controversial politician, but I could tell right away that he had a soft spot for animals. "He couldn't be all bad," I reasoned. We were just beginning to renovate the zoo and had no new exhibits to brag about, but I took Newt to meet our Asian elephant, Coca, thinking that this would be a fitting context for a Republican leader. Newt clearly enjoyed the close contact with this huge and exotic creature, the same kind that moved Alexander Pope to write: "The proper study of mankind is man, but when one regards the elephant, one wonders." Newt has since become active in sustaining the elephant's status as an endangered species.

As much as he enjoyed the elephant, he really got excited when we entered the reptile house. After about an hour there, I had to rush off for a meeting, leaving Newt in the capable hands of our reptile curator, Howard Hunt. Howard introduced Newt to every reptile, amphibian, and insect under our care, letting him handle our baby Morelet's crocodiles, selected snakes, and tortoises, and even our imposing Madagascar hissing roach. Newt grasped them all with the calm demeanor of a real zoo man. Newt Gingrich has since become one of our most consistent supporters, frequently donating to us many of the honoraria he receives for making speeches. One time I needed funds to transport a new rhino to the zoo from Czechoslovakia, but nothing was left in our budget. I called Newt, and within a few days, he sent me enough money to purchase the animal and transport it to Atlanta, not an inexpensive transaction. In return, I agreed to name the rhino after Newt's close friend Bo Callaway. Following our standard policy for naming animals, I selected an appropriate African name, Boma, which means fortress in Swahili. But the animal will always be known as Bo.

Another politician who frequented the zoo was Atlanta

mayor Andrew Young. It had been Andy's responsibility to turn the zoo around in 1984, and he often visited the improving zoo during his tenure as mayor, finding it a place for respite and healing. He attracted more attention than anyone I've walked the zoo with, except the late Marlin Perkins. With both men, we'd get only a few yards before having to make lengthy pauses for autographs and conversation. Whenever he visited us, Andy was helping to elevate our self-esteem. His special interest in African wildlife and his contacts in Kenya, Tanzania, and Rwanda also contributed to our success in many ways. We continue to value our friendship with this local leader who thinks and acts globally, just as we do.

Ted Turner has also been a globally minded partner of the zoo. Several years ago he donated a coral snake to our reptile collection, having captured the creature bare-handed near his Florida farmhouse. Being a true conservationist, he knew better than to kill the highly venomous but important predator. He also helped publicize the message that snakes are an important link in the chain of life and that we should fight to save them from extinction. In 1989, Ted addressed our regional meeting of AAZPA, when zoo colleagues from around the region visited us for the first time since the crisis of 1984. We wanted to make a good impression, and his impassioned oratory contributed greatly. On this occasion, he unveiled his "Ten Commandments for Living on Planet Earth," ideas that are now reflected in many of his enterprises, such as the animated television program "Captain Planet." These are just a few examples of the many partnerships we have formed, partnerships that have become two-way transactions in which both sides can benefit from the relationship.

For many zoos, the difference between mediocrity and excellence is the backing provided by local zoological support groups. Whether they are called "zoological societies" or "friends" associations, it is the partnership with private citizens that leads a zoo to greatness. (A list of the largest zoo associations appears in the table below.) Some great zoos are supported primarily by government—such as the National Zoo, which receives federal support—and others are primarily privately supported, but the most fiscally fit zoos receive strong support from both government and private sources. Zoo Atlanta, for example, is operated by a nonprofit management group, but we receive support from the city of Atlanta and Fulton County in the form of revenue for bond retirement. Our current operating budget is more than $9 million annually, and the city/county bond contribution amounts to more than $1 million each year. Without this support, Zoo Atlanta would operate far below its present level of quality. While the term "privatization" is used a lot these days, I much prefer the label "public/private partnership." Atlanta's private sector and local government have much to be proud of in their mutual support of Zoo Atlanta.

Zoological societies like our Friends of Zoo Atlanta (which is the third largest zoo support group in the nation) bring in millions of dollars of private money for operating and for capital construction. Nationwide, there are more than 3.6 million members of zoological societies providing such funds. But members provide more than money. In 1991, it was estimated that 20,000 dedicated volunteers worked 1.7 million hours for their local zoos. In Atlanta, more than 1,000 trained volunteers contributed more than 50,000 hours at the zoo. One example is our annual "Beastly Feast," where in 1992 they raised nearly $300,000 in just one night. And, community corporate leaders volunteer their time to help raise more money for our annual fund and capital campaigns. So, we are twice blessed. This is the public/private partnership at its best!

In Atlanta, it was also the zoological society that led the fight to revitalize the zoo, and this has happened in many communities. All too frequently, however, city zoos and their support groups struggle with each other over leadership during hard times. This makes it difficult to operate the zoo, since two heads are competing for power and

TOP TEN ZOOS AND AQUARIUMS BY MEMBERSHIP

1. San Diego Zoological Society	200,000
2. New York Zoological Society	95,000
3. Zoo Atlanta	**53,863**
4. Henry Doorly Zoo	52,000
5. Los Angeles Zoo	49,000
6. Philadelphia Zoo	48,000
7. Cincinnati Zoo	42,000
8. Audubon Park Zoo	35,000
9. Chicago Zoological Society	25,000
10. Baltimore Aquarium	25,000

(All data from AAZPA's *Zoological Parks and Aquariums in the Americas*, published by the American Society of Zoological Parks and Aquariums, 1992–93.)

authority. The solution to this kind of conflict is to unify the zoo and its support organization. The recent "merger" in Atlanta of our zoo and the Friends of Zoo Atlanta, for example, is proving to be one of the most significant events in our history. To make the merger successful, the Friends had to subordinate their identity to that of the zoo, but the process was made reasonably painless through the good will of our society leadership, under the skillful direction of executive director Clare Richardson. Our merger can only be regarded as an extraordinary act of friendship and trust between two true partners. Now we have twice the strength with which to promote and support our cause. The best zoos have big operating budgets. The combined strength of Zoo Atlanta and the Friends puts us in the top ten of America's zoos as measured by the size of their operating budgets.

At Zoo Atlanta our earliest successes in promoting ourselves came through the media. Our reputation, as disseminated through newspapers, radio, and television, was so bad when I started in 1984 that this really had to be our first marketing priority. When I arrived, the zoo was on the beat of every investigative reporter in Atlanta, and many from outside the city as well. One member of the staff even had a regular pipeline to investigative reporters of the *Atlanta Journal and Constitution*, and other staff routinely communicated directly with reporters. The press may have been doing its job, in the general sense, but the published stories were often full of inaccuracies, making the situation look even worse. For example, an early news item alleged that a zookeeper had eaten some of the zoo's rabbits. There was some truth to this story, since the culprit was a city maintenance worker who obtained surplus rabbits from a zoo curator. But no zookeeper ever consumed zoo rabbits, even in those dark days. Nevertheless, newspapers continue to repeat this factual error when the zoo's history is recalled. It may seem like a small detail, but our keepers continue to be embarrassed by it. Of course, it was a terrible mistake for a curator to give the rab-

BIG LEAGUE ZOOS BY SIZE OF OPERATING BUDGET

1.	San Diego Zoological Zoo & Wild Animal Park	$60 million
2.	New York Zoological Park	$29 million
3.	Chicago Zoological Park (Brookfield Zoo)	$23 million
4.	Metro Toronto	$19 million
5.	National Zoo	$16 million
6.	Los Angeles Zoo	$13.5 million
7.	Milwaukee Zoo	$12.5 million
8.	Calgary Zoo	$10.5 million
9.	**Zoo Atlanta**	**$10 million**
10.	Minnesota Zoo	$9.5 million

(AAZPA's *Zoological Parks and Aquariums in the Americas*, 1992–93. Zoo Atlanta data from 1993 operating budget. All data to nearest half million.)

bits away in the first place, and I am proud to say that something this stupid could never happen today.

Still, there has been an up-side to all this media attention. We were newsworthy, and we had the ear of the media. As a result, we were in a unique position to deliver some good news, and good messages, that the public could not ignore. The press provided the catalyst for the zoo's crisis to become a public problem, and it also became a driving force behind the turnaround in our reputation. To facilitate this, I resolved to be accessible to the media, so that they could get the very best information, and to always be truthful with them, even when the truth was painful. It worked. "Watch Terry Maple closely," read an editorial just a couple weeks after my appointment. "He is about to demonstrate what a little clear-headedness can do."

Our zoo vision is truly revolutionary, and we experience it in the events and innovations of every passing day. We promote this vision with enthusiasm and zeal, but we understand that a vision must be sharpened and tested if it is going to last. Tom Peters said it best in his bestseller *Thriving on Chaos*:

> Visions are aesthetic and moral—as well as strategically sound. Visions come from within—as well as from the outside. They are personal—and group-centered. Developing a vision and values is a messy, artistic process. Living it convincingly is a passionate one, without any doubt.

As we solved each problem at the zoo, little by little, we had new tales to tell. These new tales were every bit as interesting as the ones about our fall from grace, and the press used them. In 1986, for example, the *Atlanta Journal and Constitution* ran a contest for us, raising money to buy a new elephant for the zoo. "Let's buy the zoo a new baby elephant," read the headline, so dramatically different from those just two years ago, which frequently advocated closing the zoo. Children from around the region donated enough money to buy an elephant, and Food Giant employees donated an additional amount to buy a second one. A total of $57,000 was raised in this way to purchase Victoria and Zambezi.

We were a good story and we have continued to be a good story ever since. The opening of our rain forest exhibit, for example, was covered by newspapers, magazines, and television stations across the country and around the world. Even *Travel & Leisure* magazine, doing a story about visiting gorillas in the wild in Africa, included a piece on our exhibits as the next best thing to the wild:

> Grabbing a plane for Africa isn't on everyone's travel agenda, so the closest many of us will get to seeing a gorilla in its native habitat is a rerun of a Dian Fossey documentary. Or that's how it was before Zoo Atlanta opened its lowland gorilla exhibit in June.

Still, we were careful not to run wild with the publicity, not to create hype without substance. We spent a good deal of time and energy developing a good, credible zoo, so we didn't have to exaggerate. We simply tried to get reporters to write true stories about our successful staff, animal births, new arrivals and other significant events, our conservation and education programs, and our innovative new exhibits. Sometimes the truth is more powerful than fiction, to wit the following news clip about Boma the rhino, by reporter David Nordan:

> Interested in rare, endangered species? How about a black rhino that likes Vivaldi? You wouldn't believe it to look at this hulking, 4,000-pound body with the primeval stare and fierce, curved horn, but . . . the music of the 18th Century Italian composer appears to be the great beast's favorite.

A ROLE FOR SCIENCE IN THE ZOO

We are unhappy about the magnitude, if not the excellence, of research within parks. If the zoo is a storehouse for scientific investigators, why then is this storehouse not more uniformly exploited? In my opinion, it is primarily because it is difficult to "sell" the idea of basic research.

Kurt Benirschke, **Research in Zoos and Aquariums**

My own scientific inspiration was first nurtured both in my own backyard and in the zoo. I spent my first five years on a dairy farm, surrounded by large creatures and a father who was an animal man, milking cows and raising chickens, rabbits, and geese. My mother raised parakeets, finches, and lovebirds for many years, and our house was always filled with the requisite dogs, cats, and occasional exotic creatures. My next home, in the southern San Diego suburb of Chula Vista, backed up to the hill country where wildlife was abundant. Our neighborhood games revolved around the themes of exploration and archeology. We were always looking for creatures not yet discovered by science, spending much of our time in a place we called "fossil canyon." We were sure there were monsters in fossil canyon, and, as it turns out, we were right. Just a few years ago, after the area was uncovered by developers, archeologists discovered there an abundance of 13- to 16-million-year-old mammal and reptile remains. One of these creatures was identified as an oreodont, an extinct, pig-like beast. The proud archeologists announced that theirs were the first fossils ever discovered in these rocks. But I knew the truth: back in 1955, working with just a screwdriver and a scout knife, I had pulled out a fist-sized ancient clam from the canyon.

The San Diego Zoo was another superb location for scientific inspiration during my boyhood. My grandmother would pack a lunch and the whole family would spend the day in Balboa Park, where the zoo and its huge collection are located. Every time we entered those gates, I would dash in the direction of the giant snakes, exhorting my family to follow. The boas and pythons were particularly fascinating to me, and I liked to study all the lizards, especially the gila monster. (The gila monster was an animal I worried about while playing in the hills. We never encountered one, but we did see plenty of horned lizards and I fantasized about them being small dinosaurs.) So, years later when I began to study animals in earnest, I knew the zoo was an ideal site.

There were just a few research projects undertaken at the Atlanta Zoo before our turnaround, but they were good bases to build upon. For example, several studies had been undertaken in the reptile department since 1965. The best work derived from Howard Hunt's long-term studies of American alligators in the Okefenokee. And since the Yerkes Primate Center had located great apes at the zoo, some investigators had observed these animals in a scientific way. It was one such investigation that first attracted me to the zoo in 1975. My favorite critters, the orangutans, looked like the best research opportunity in the zoo at the time. A group of seven orangs had been housed together, an unusual arrangement for a zoo. I learned later that the animals had been brought there for scientific observation by a Yerkes/Georgia Tech scientist, Dr. Richard K. Davenport. Dr. Davenport, who had studied this species in Borneo, had hoped to complement his field studies with observations of a captive group. By the time I arrived in

Atlanta, however, Dr. Davenport was no longer observing them, opening up a perfect niche for me.

This group of orangs was an incredibly rich source of activity for study. On that first visit to the zoo, I witnessed something very unusual: paternal behavior. Adult male orangutans had been thought to be essentially solitary creatures, and no accounts of male parental behavior had been documented before. I stood transfixed by the sight of this big male actively playing, rough-and-tumble style, with his four-year-old male offspring. As they rolled about, play biting, grunting, and clearly having a wonderful time, I couldn't wait to share this discovery with someone who could appreciate it. (We later found out that it was the youngster who was the primary initiator of these play-bouts, but the adult male was certainly vigorous in reciprocating.)

I returned one day later with my first Emory graduate student, Evan Zucker, and observed several lengthy copulations. We knew that in other great apes, mating behavior was cyclic—hormones that are produced in the female at mid-cycle induce copulation. But here, we were seeing copulation much more frequently. We arranged for two adult pairs of orangutans to be housed at the zoo (requiring the acquisition of an additional adult male) so that another student, Beth Dennon, could carry out a study of this phenomenon. I could scarcely believe it when Beth told me that one of the females was exhibiting aggressive sexual interest in a male, since this behavior had not been documented. After I confirmed her findings, we decided to capture it on film and continue recording data. This became the first documented account of the behavior known as "proceptivity" in orangutans. Orangutan social behavior proved to be a fascinating area for research, so we continued working on the topic for several years, publishing many papers. Almost every week, I received calls from curators and keepers at zoos around the country, wanting to know more about our work. This is what eventually led to the 1980 publication of my second book, *Orangutan Behavior*.

Orangutans are truly wonderful creatures, easy to appreciate but difficult to decipher. They are stoic by comparison to their close relatives the gorillas and chimpanzees. Robert and Ada Yerkes regarded the orangutan as lacking ambition, determination, and energy. As they stated in their classic book *The Great Apes*, "The orang-utan, inactive, or sluggish, gives the impression of stolidity, brooding, depression, melancholy. It is phlegmatic and its attitude and behavior often suggests [*sic*] pensiveness and pessimism."

As the largest primate that lives an arboreal life, the orangutan is cautious and slow moving; and rightly so, since orangs occasionally fall, and they have been known to suffer serious injuries, including broken limbs. Slow, deliberate movement, in captivity and in the wild, is a primary characteristic of an orangutan. Prepared for a life in trees, orangs are also grasping animals, using all four limbs to sustain movement in a complex network of limbs and vines. When orangs fight, they grasp tenaciously and bite. This characteristic is what makes them so much more dangerous than other apes. Ape keepers are unanimous in rating the orangutan as the ape they would least like to meet in the dark alley of an unlocked cage.

Orangutans have a strong propensity toward a solitary life. They just flat out like to be alone, especially big males. In the wild, they express their solitary nature by traveling singly or in small, transient social units of two to three animals. Males meet females to mate, while females sometimes travel with mature female offspring. The unit that scientists most commonly observe is a female with dependent young. Unlike gorillas, they do not congregate in family groups. Insight into this solitary nature is hard to come by, but Sy Montgomery's characterization after she spent time among Bornean orangutans is a choice one:

> Orangutans never let you hold the delusion that they need you. They can just walk by you and never look back. They're very engaging animals, but you have to push yourself on them. The

> relationship is like 70 percent you, 30 percent them. Watching them, I realized I could never be one of them. Maybe you can be a chimpanzee. Maybe you can be a gorilla. But you can't be an orangutan. . . . That's what gives them their majesty, their nobility—they don't need anybody.

This independent spirit is an admirable feature, and this may be why they seem to adjust so well to life in captivity. No matter how decrepit their facilities, orangutans deal with it. Often they simply take their environment apart, and this is the other ubiquitous feature of their personality: they are the most creatively manipulative of the apes. Zoo people acknowledge their expertise as the zoo world's most talented "escape artists."

Zoo directors are not supposed to have "favorite" animals. By this unwritten rule, the director must be evenhanded and dispense affection to his or her collection equally. Long after his retirement, the great director Heini Hediger confessed to me that his favorite zoo animals were the hippos and tree frogs. I took great pleasure in videotaping Hediger at Zoo Zürich while he hand-fed the hippos he once knew so well. It was a uniquely moving reunion between a man and his beasts, and the affection was clearly mutual.

Hediger gives me courage to admit to my favorites. I like long-legged birds, storks and cranes, and I like rhinos and elephants. I am especially fond of hedgehogs and hyraxes, and my favorite reptile is Georgia's indigo snake. Giant tortoises fascinate me, and I like all forms of lizards, especially iguanas. Still, I will always be an ape man, and my favorite apes are orangutans. For me, Sy Montgomery's words express my precise feelings: "We westerners aspire to be orangutans. If you look at the end goal of our culture, it's to be totally independent of everybody—spouses, parents, children; an orangutan."

Today at Zoo Atlanta, orangutans still loom large in our research programs. They are, in fact, our most studied taxon. For example, Lorraine Perkins, Zoo Atlanta's conservation biologist, has documented the effects of the environment on orangutan behavior. In her master's thesis for Georgia Tech's School of Psychology, which was later published in *Zoo Biology*, she determined that the best predictors of orangutan activity are the combination and number of animals in a group, the amount of usable surface area and spatial volume in their habitat, and the number of movable objects available to them. This finding corroborated our longstanding belief that spatial complexity contributes to the psychological well-being of captive animals. And, those exhibits that successfully simulate nature are the most likely to result in appropriate behaviors by the animals.

Of course, our continuing work with orangutans is possible only because of the Yerkes Primate Center, which loaned the zoo twelve orangutans and sixteen gorillas in 1988. The gorillas, too, became the object of scientific investigation. One study, conducted by Dr. Jackie Ogden (who is now at the San Diego Zoo's Center for Research on Endangered Species), investigated the behavior of all sixteen gorillas as they adjusted to their new, outdoor enclosures. Based on 451 hours of behavioral data, Ogden reported that the animals were initially cautious and that it took about six months for their exploratory behavior to drop off. This indicates that the animals were challenged by the naturalistic features of the environment. However, we observed that they spent a good amount of their time in the back areas of the enclosure, which were similar to their previous, cage-like surroundings. We concluded that while gorillas benefit from naturalistic environments, they may also be comforted by "familiar features." Perhaps some familiar features should be retained, even in the most advanced natural habitats.

Our animal research at the zoo will at some point concern almost every species in the collection. Reptiles and primates are our most studied taxa, but other critters are getting more attention as we attract new collaborators. One question that has intrigued us for many years concerns flamingos and their breeding habits. When we built our new flamingo exhibit in 1986, our curator of birds (the late Guy Farnell) advised me that it would take a lot of birds to ensure breeding. "How many?" I asked. "Sixty birds," he replied. I couldn't imagine sixty birds in our enclosure; it didn't seem large enough. But, trusting in the curator's judgment, we ordered sixty birds. And, sure enough, they fit in the enclosure perfectly and began producing eggs as soon as they were mature.

Today, our research leader, Dr. Beth Stevens, continues to study these birds, as well as those at the National Zoo. Her careful observations and recordings of the birds' vocalizations have led to many interesting findings. For example, she has isolated a number of flamingo signals and sounds and observed how these affect interactions within the group. She has shown that only flamingos in large groups, which is how they live in the wild, successfully pair up, mate, lay and guard their eggs, and rear their offspring. So Stevens has now documented a phenomenon based on a curator's hunch.

Many of our staff also study animals in their wild habitats, sometimes in cooperation with researchers from other institutions. These studies have ramifications both for the survival of these species in the wild and for their management in captivity. Dr. Debra Forthman, for example, has put together a project with a longtime zoo volunteer (Wayne Esarove) to study a herd of orphaned elephants in Rwanda's Akagera National Park. These animals were moved from their natal herd back in 1975 and presented a unique opportunity to see how they are faring without the adult female leadership they normally depend on. The researchers also plan to extend the focus of their study to include the establishment of a broader program of conservation-oriented "eco-tourism" in Akagera. Such ecologically oriented tourism programs can help the local economy.

Our general curator, Dr. Dietrich Schaaf, has conducted an important series of field studies of the drill, a highly endangered forest baboon. Traveling to Bioko, an island off the west coast of Africa, Schaaf assessed the numbers and status of the drills and is now initiating a long-term study of their behavior and ecology. This information may eventually help save the species in the wild and is already being used to encourage better reproduction among captive drills.

We also frequently study human animals—the visitors to our zoo. At the National Zoo in Washington, D.C., Dale Marcellini initiated such a series of studies. Using standard observational techniques, he simply tracked the people who entered the zoo, estimating the age and sex distribution and group composition, and recorded their behavior. He discovered that the average visitor to the National Zoo stayed for two and one-half hours, but spent only fourteen minutes in the reptile house. Throughout the zoo, the biggest animals drew the best: in the reptile house, the giant snakes had staying power, while elsewhere, the pandas, elephants, and gorillas got the lion's share of attention. (Lions themselves, though, were viewed for an average of only one minute, while pandas got five!) There were also some surprises. Visitors preferred watching bats more than eagles, and they largely ignored the hoofed stock. Zoo directors and their business managers pay attention to such telling research.

As we rebuild Zoo Atlanta, we have tried to learn such things as whether people actually read our signage and which exhibits they find the most compelling. I conducted my first visitor study at the Sacramento Zoo in 1974, in collaboration with my former student Dr. Michael P. Hoff, and later replicated the procedures in Atlanta. What we were interested in was the propensity of certain people to avoid reptiles. In our studies, we found that females refused to enter zoo reptile houses more often than males, and that they spent less time within the facility when they did choose to enter. We also discovered that teenagers of both sexes were the most willing to enter reptile houses and spent significantly more time inside than other age groups. These findings generally supported previous research indicating a gender difference in "fear of snakes." Although animal phobias tend to appear at an early age, teenagers, it seems, behaved as if they were not afraid, entering reptile houses in spite of their fear. It also appeared to us that the female teenagers overcame their fear as a function of their attraction to male peers.

Most recently, we at Zoo Atlanta have even begun to study ourselves, which is something I had wanted to do from the beginning. During my first week as zoo director, I realized that the staff had essentially lost hope. As a psychologist, I wanted to document this state of mind, to measure it as a baseline from which to evaluate later improvements. But I couldn't bring myself to do it. I was sure that the morale was so low that no scale could measure it anyway, so I deferred this self-study. I understood that the zoo staff at that time needed to look ahead, to envision and welcome change. To facilitate this, I invited Gary Clarke, director of the "World Famous Topeka Zoo" and the most beloved leader in the zoo industry, to visit us. I asked Gary to give a motivational talk to my staff, telling them that if they worked hard and became a team, they could turn the zoo around. It was too early for my staff to believe in me, but I hoped they would believe in Gary. His enthusiasm and confidence made a real difference in this early stage of our recovery.

In 1991, I was finally brave enough to commission a real survey of ourselves. Using the expertise of Georgia Tech psychologist Jack Feldman and graduate student Christine Shoob, we studied the work "climate" within the zoo, the overall mood of our organization and its staff. We wanted to know whether our work climate was positive or negative and identify any organizational problems within the zoo. We also wanted to determine whether our organizational climate was successfully encouraging research activity, and to measure the extent to which our staff accepted our educational, conservation, and scientific mission. The resulting study has been a valuable tool for our managers. It revealed that a high percentage of the staff felt positive about their jobs, coworkers, and supervisors, the teamwork within their departments, the quality of their work, and the mission of the zoo. However, we also learned that there was dissatisfaction with pay and opportunities for advancement within the zoo. We continue to address these and other problems identified by our consulting psychologists at Georgia Tech.

From time to time, zoo professionals argue about whether basic research or applied research should have the greatest priority in the zoo. Most agree that applied studies have a higher priority because they provide quick payoffs as their results are applied to situations in the zoo. There are many understudied animals, and practical information about their behavior and other factors is in great demand, as I have discovered from the many zoo curators and keepers who have called me for advice about great ape behavior. But basic research is not really so different. It provides information that will be applied in some way, at some time. For example, studies of the endocrine secretions of apes will provide information that will help us monitor the course of pregnancy, which is a rather important application. However, just the existence of this argument shows how far zoos have come. When I first came to the Atlanta Zoo, some scientific research had been conducted, but not in any organizational way.

My favorite example of an applied zoo research project involves Zoo Atlanta's new gorilla exhibits, which were being visited by record crowds in 1988. Unfortunately, many of the new residents spent a lot of time in the most distant locations of their spacious habitats and were very difficult to see. Visitors began to complain, but our research department was already on the job. Dr. Duane Jackson, one of our visiting scientists, compiled data on numbers of visitors viewing one of the main habitats, during different times of the day. He then correlated these data with information on the gorillas' use of the habitats gathered by my former student, Dr. Jackie Ogden. His results confirmed my worst suspicions: the gorillas were least visible at the time of day when the greatest numbers of visitors were there to see them. It was a nearly perfect inverse correlation! Armed with these scientific data, however, we made changes in the gorillas' management to counteract the problem. These included sequencing the times at which each gorilla group was let outside in the morning and inducing them to the front of their habitats by providing food during peak visitation hours.

But science hasn't always been easy, and scientific projects are still very hard to sustain in the zoo. Yet they have helped make Zoo Atlanta and other zoos into much greater places. With their less-than-noble history, and their roots in the circus industry, zoos like ours have traditionally held little appeal for scientists. Early in their career, comparative psychologists Harry F. Harlow and Abraham Maslow made good use of zoos, but only to see whether the social relations of monkeys provided clues to understanding human behavior. At about the same time, in Switzerland, Heini Hediger began to develop a unique new discipline that he labeled "zoo biology." Hediger defined this new science as "everything in the zoo which is biologically relevant . . . from zoology to human psychology and from ecology to pathology."

Although Hediger had defined the field of zoo biology, the profession still resisted science. It occurred to me in the early 1980s that a scientific journal might contribute to the development of a scientific identity for zoos and aquariums. Talk about the need for a zoo journal had circulated in the zoo community for years, but no one had been able to make it work. For fifty years, the New York Zoological Society had published an excellent journal, *Zoologica*, but it ceased publication in 1973 due to a lack of interest within the profession. There just wasn't enough good research being conducted in zoos to fill each issue.

In 1981, while I was working at the Audubon Zoo in New Orleans, I concluded that there might be just enough "true believers" to put together an editorial board for such a journal, and enough outside academics to lend assistance. With encouragement from Heini Hediger, a small cadre of science-minded colleagues, and the approval of the board of the American Society of Zoological Parks and Aquariums, the journal *Zoo Biology* was launched in 1982. I edited the journal for the next seven years, and my hopes that it would encourage more research and more research departments came to fruition. In the first issue I wrote:

> The growing importance of scientific activity in zoological gardens is widely acknowledged. Zoo scientists need a publication outlet that conforms to the traditional rigors of scholarship and peer review. At the same time, the many professional issues that demand our attention require a flexible format and broad participation. . . . The journal will offer data and theory, but it is additionally obligated to solve problems and suggest innovations.

That first issue, eighty-four pages long, contained three behavioral studies, two studies in reproductive biology, an evaluation of computer technology, and two book reviews. We were soon able to attract scientific papers of the highest quality from all over the world.

Today, under the editorship of Dr. Donald G. Lindburg of the San Diego Zoo, *Zoo Biology*'s publication standards are tougher than ever, and the journal continues to flourish as an elite outlet for zoo research. Dr. Lindburg's recent examination of the first seven years of the journal revealed that zoo studies ran the gamut from investigations of animal reproduction and behavior, to facility design, husbandry, and animal management. Thus, much of the work is directly applicable to the design of zoo exhibits. In a recent survey of zoos, Ted Finlay and I discovered that nearly 70 percent of our respondents were able to document recent research, while nearly half of them claimed to be expanding their research programs. As academics, we were also very interested in the finding that zoos affiliated with universities were the most productive in research.

Given the success of *Zoo Biology* and the importance of science in the zoo revolution, it is surprising that so many zoo administrations still struggle with the role of science. A few zoos made research a priority early in their history—such as London, Antwerp, Amsterdam, New York, and San Diego—and these institutions are among some of the most credible zoos of our time. Today, science is recognized as one of the four basic directives that good zoological parks in America must support (along with conservation, recreation, and education), but the road to acceptance has been bumpy. AAZPA has reflected this uncertainty, as the word "research" has appeared, disappeared, and reappeared in its masthead slogan over the past twenty years. Most recently it has resurfaced with a new, albeit redundant label: "scientific studies." One reason for this reticence is the confusing of our scientific interests with those of biomedicine, in which animals are used as a model in the study of human medicine. In contrast, zoo biology is the study of animals in their own right, both in zoos and in the wild.

Aside from these historical and philosophical difficulties, zoo research programs have also confronted organizational and economic barriers. Zoos never have quite enough money to do all of the things they must, and that doesn't always leave many dollars for research. Zoo leaders report that they want to do more research, but that they can't afford to pay for it. At Zoo Atlanta, for instance, we have found that we must raise extra money to support our research projects, since our standard operating budget for research is modest. We frequently ask our donors and members to help support individual projects. And we're always applying for research grants from outside agencies and foundations. Nevertheless, we keep trying, because science is one of the mainstays of our redevelopment.

These economic pressures are exacerbated by the difficulties of establishing a comfortable place and policy for a research department within a zoo. At Zoo Atlanta, even though we rebuilt the zoo practically from scratch, we have at times struggled with the role and scope of our scientific programs, as have most zoos. Science was a key theme in our platform of renewal, and we established a conservation and research department in 1987, but the programs didn't really take off until 1989, when we reached a "critical mass" of research personnel—three full-time and six part-time staff. The full-time staff today includes a research leader (with a Ph.D. in biology), a program coordinator (with a Ph.D. in psychology) and a conservation biologist (a Ph.D. candidate). All of them have strong publication records and research experience. Most of the part-timers have been graduate students on part-time stipends.

However, there was no way this small but wonderful staff could do everything we wanted to do, so we began to develop relationships with outside collaborators. One way we did this was by establishing a "visiting scientist" program, in which we bring university faculty (currently from Morehouse College, Dalton College, and Georgia Tech) to the zoo for the summer, paying them a modest salary to conduct research. This inducement in turn has led to year-round research participation by these faculty and their students. As a result, this program now boasts a small cadre of working university researchers, at a total cost of $30,000 per year.

Indeed, cooperation with universities has become a major modus operandi for zoo research departments. And zoos provide something for universities as well: unique and diverse collections of wild animals to study, plus opportunities for public service. In fact, in 1985, Dr. Donna Hardy of California State University at Northridge started the Consortium of Aquariums, Universities and Zoos (CAUZ), an organization dedicated to helping zoos and universities work together. "This kind of collaboration can bring together the valuable, and sometimes underutilized, resources of these institutions as well as increase the quantity and quality of research at zoos and aquariums," she proclaimed. She is absolutely correct.

At Zoo Atlanta, one of our most unique university relationships has been with the College of Architecture at Georgia Tech, because it involves both research and teaching. Dr. Jean Wineman and I have partnered as teachers for the past fourteen years, but she has also conducted research at the zoo as one of our first visiting scientists. In one of her projects, she analyzed the spatial and visual characteristics of the zoo in terms of its stated educational goals. She wanted to determine whether the contrast between the old zoo master plan (from 1950) and the new plan (from 1985) would indicate differences in prevailing educational philosophies. Her conclusion was revealing:

> The social and entertainment focus of the old zoo . . . emphasizes people-oriented spaces and animals on display. In the new zoo . . . individual and small group experience is emphasized. Intimate spaces are the focal points where visitors experience animals in . . . natural habitats. Educational impact is heightened through the individualized and unexpected nature of the experience. In this way, spatial organization assumes an integral role in achieving the institution's educational goals.

Dr. Wineman's research and teaching are just part of her contribution. She also serves on our Technical Advisory Board, to provide advice to the zoo director and the veterinarian. In this capacity, she has provided expert consultation on handicapped access and on programming work space for our new administrative center. Recently, she collaborated with members of the zoo staff to obtain a grant from the National Endowment for the Arts so the zoo could host a workshop on children's zoo design. When the experts convened in Atlanta, we were able to generate new ideas to effect the programming of forthcoming exhibits for children. Could we do all this without the university? Maybe so, but I don't think we could do it as well.

In order to ensure smooth operations between our zoo and our many university partners, we often exchange "memoranda of understanding," which outline the responsibilities and commitments of each participating institution. For example, our relationship with Georgia Tech's College of Architecture is backed up by a document that calls for a "joint program of research, education, and technical assistance." The document does not specify the details of how we work together, but rather identifies areas where collaboration is desirable and mutually beneficial. This approach, in which the relationship is clearly documented, is strongly advocated by AAZPA's conservation coordinator, Dr. Michael Hutchins.

We also recommend an approval process for each project, which is especially important for those from outside investigators. Our procedure involves evaluation of each proposal by a team of zoo staff, distribution to our Technical Advisory Board for "humane care" input, and final disposition by the director. The approved project is then given to an appointed staff manager for monitoring. Proposals are evaluated on the basis of their scientific merit, conservation potential, and educational benefits. Additional factors include the project's value to management, its relationship to the zoo's mission, and its effects on the zoo's animal collection and resources.

Many years ago I compiled a list of suggestions for zoo scientists to make sure their work in the zoo goes as smoothly as possible. It was based on the many mistakes I made as a novice zoo biologist, naive to the ways of the zoo world.

A ZOO SCIENTIST'S CREDO

1. Explain project objectives to zoo staff in a concise, lucid, written form.
2. Relate the importance of the project to the zoo mission.
3. Become an active member of the local zoo society.
4. Explain research methods to participating curators and keepers.
5. Use the curators and keepers as resources. Learn what they know about the animals.
6. Arrive for work on a reliable schedule.
7. Acknowledge the participation of zoo staff.
8. Provide regular progress reports.
9. Explain zoo rules and regulations to any student assistants, and enforce them.
10. Bring projects to a clean and final conclusion.
11. Submit findings for publication as soon as possible, and seek co-authors from among zoo collaborators.
12. Send the zoo sufficient copies of any publications.

Within the zoo, we have learned that it is important for someone to be accountable for research, enforcement of the written guidelines, and the circulation of research findings throughout the zoo. In addition, if a zoo is to become truly scientific, the research department must be elevated to the highest levels of decision making. At Zoo Atlanta, we have empowered the conservation and research department by giving the research leader senior-management status and a reporting relationship to the director. In our organization, the research leader is on an equal footing with the veterinarian and the general curator. As a result, research is discussed in senior staff meetings, along with marketing, finance, and other topics. This helps sustain the key role of this important department.

It is also essential for the research department to have the support of other zoo staff, and vice versa. A research

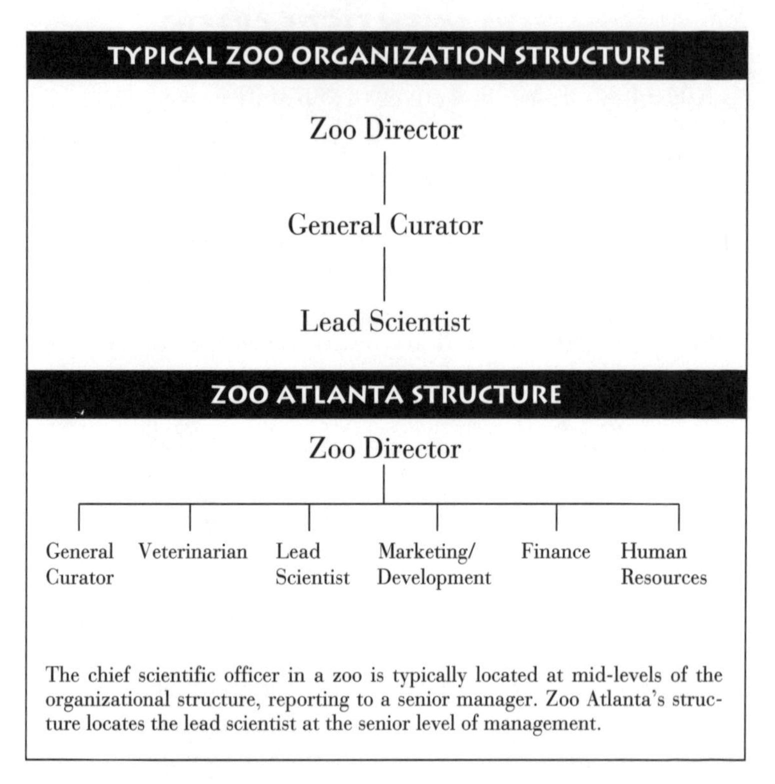

The chief scientific officer in a zoo is typically located at mid-levels of the organizational structure, reporting to a senior manager. Zoo Atlanta's structure locates the lead scientist at the senior level of management.

unit is only as good as its day-to-day interactions with other key personnel, particularly keepers and curators. And, staff outside the research department should be encouraged not only to assist the scientists but to initiate studies of their own, using the research department for support. A good example of this at Zoo Atlanta is the collaboration of our curator of reptiles, Howard Hunt, and Dr. Jackie Ogden, formerly of our research department. Hunt had been gathering data on alligators in the Okefenokee Swamp for years. Ogden was able to help him analyze these data statistically, and she found that log-linear analysis provided the best answers to Hunt's research questions. The analysis determined, for example, that nest sites guarded by alligators experienced a significantly lower rate of predation than unguarded nest sites. In this project, a seasoned curator/naturalist was ably assisted by a computer-friendly psychologist, and the two collaborators published their findings in the prestigious *Journal of Herpetology*. Zoo science works best when scientists, caretakers, and curators work together as equal partners in the research process.

The goals and methods should be carefully explained before a project begins, and the rewards—such as publication credit—should be shared whenever possible. Our scientists are held responsible for the overall success of our scientific programs, and for ensuring that other staff participate. Even our registrar has a role in research. Her careful maintenance of animal records means that we have an archival database to draw upon, which is necessary for studies of trends in mortality, diseases, and so forth. One way to promote this type of intra-zoo collaboration is to try to recruit staff who have a special interest and background in research, and to provide some scientific training for those already in the zoo.

Establishing a research department within the zoo organization is just the beginning, however. The breadth of the research niche must be considered carefully. How many other functions within the zoo should it touch? Should research be in some way connected to everything we do? At Zoo Atlanta, our research philosophy has developed to the point where almost every aspect of the zoo is fair game for research. In addition to studying animals in the zoo and in the wild, our research projects have also studied how animals use the new exhibits, how visitors perceive the zoo, and even how we ourselves, as an organization, are functioning. The zoo's research unit is one that can serve virtually all zoo departments, even the business side. The research department can help procure and analyze marketing data, and can even help with computer programs to aid our record keeping. Our management style can be made thoroughly objective because it is based on science, the golden thread that touches every aspect of our organization.

As much as zoo research has advanced in recent years, there is probably no zoo where the ultimate goal has been reached: the complete integration of research, education, and conservation. Zoo educators rarely talk to zoo biologists, and one program often does not benefit from the existence of another. In a perfect zoo world, the work of conservation biologists would be the curriculum for conservation educators: Scientists would participate in the development of educational programs and share their knowledge with those who teach. One thing we have done at Zoo Atlanta to further this goal is to bring the research, education, and conservation activities together under one umbrella, which we have named the Conservation Action Resource Center, or Conservation ARC. We now hope to establish a major endowment to keep the ARC afloat. We anticipate that the future successes of our center will inspire similar restructuring at other zoos.

As conservation leaders, zoo directors must elevate the standing of research. Our conservation and educational efforts are knowledge based. To sustain a respectable population of talented and well-trained zoo biologists, we have to get serious about science. We can and should do more and better research in our zoos. For example, an expanding network of zoo biologists and collaborating scientists from universities, primate centers, and research institutes may be the salvation of AAZPA's crucial Species Survival Programs, which manage our captive populations of endangered species. Unfortunately, solutions to our pressing demographic, husbandry, propagation, and management problems are being promulgated at the pace of a lethargic gastropod. A small cadre of America's dedicated zoo professionals are working overtime on microcomputers, but every zoo needs to contribute more human and financial resources to these problems. In the short run, we may need to recruit more technical volunteers just to catch up.

A recent study by Dr. Ben Beck and Ted Power at the National Zoo illustrates the type of applied research that zoos need to encourage. The two behavioral scientists used questionnaires to collect standardized biographies of every gorilla in North America. Searching for factors associated with reproductive success or failure, the authors concluded that many cases of reproductive failure are due to deficits in sexual behavior, influenced by a lack of early social experience with other gorillas. Interestingly, and in contrast to other studies of captive apes, Beck and Power did not find an association between maternal competence and rearing experience. This type of research is extremely valuable to zoo managers and should be the first priority for funding.

One of the unspoken deficiencies in zoo research is the dearth of dedicated talent. The problems we must solve are enormously challenging, and bright people are needed to do it. Yet, we plod along too often with staff who are poorly prepared to deal with these problems. At Zoo Atlanta we have recruited top-quality scientists and curators in greater numbers, and I feel this is essential for a modern zoo. We must identify individuals with the technical skills to push the conservation agenda forward. I really believe these jobs require a Ph.D.-level education, like professorships and most research positions. In addition, too many zoos relegate research to the middle levels of the management team and offer salaries at levels well below the competitive rate in academia. We must seek out first-rate talent to fill senior-level positions in the zoo. We also need to have stronger and more dedicated research participation from other players in the zoo, such as the animal managers, although these staff are already up to their ears in day-to-day responsibilities. Science must be elevated among our zoo priorities.

Local universities may be the answer. Although Zoo Atlanta is one of the most networked zoos in the nation, we are far from exhausting the possibilities in Atlanta. Every zoo can develop meaningful relationships to universities, and a simple meeting with a department chair or dean can start the ball rolling. Faculty are a tremendous resource for collaboration and technical assistance. Relationships to local universities can also provide access to library resources, computer services, medical illustration, and other campus facilities. At Zoo Atlanta, our staff have also benefitted from these relationships by being able to obtain training for advanced degrees. The most profound benefit of all is the enhanced credibility we gain from our association with esteemed institutions of higher learning. Heini Hediger expressed surprise at the failure of most zoos and universities to develop complementary relationships:

> Every university which boasts a botanical institute will also have—in Europe at any rate—a botanical garden. Yet I know of no zoological institute which is properly complemented by a zoological garden. To the best of my knowledge, there is, in fact, not one single university zoo.

Once a research program is seeded, zoo directors must insist on two outcomes: high-quality publications produced with reasonable frequency by research staff and affiliates, and routine submissions for research grants from outside foundations and agencies. These are the criteria by which research departments must be judged and rewarded, as they are in the academic world. One can make some judgments on the strength of scientific programs from the following:

TOP TEN ZOOS BY 1992 SCIENTIFIC PUBLICATIONS

	Zoo	Publications
1.	National Zoological Park	85
2.	New York Zoological Park	60
3.	San Diego Zoo	46
4.	Brookfield Zoo	10
5.	Cincinnati Zoo	10
6.	Sea World, Inc.	10
7.	St. Louis Zoo	9
8.	Dallas Zoo	8
9.	Zoo Atlanta	7
10.	Henry Doorly Zoo	6
	Sacramento Zoo	6

(*AAZPA Annual Report on Conservation & Science*, 1991–92. Only refereed publications were counted.)

We at Zoo Atlanta are proud to have made this "top ten" list, but we won't be really happy until the list is much longer, with every zoo participating fully, and until the numbers are much larger. Only then will science—a major part of the revolution—have found its true role at the zoo.

TEACHERS WITH TALONS

A man can sit for hours before an aquarium and stare into it as into the flames of an open fire or the rushing waters of a torrent. All conscious thought is happily lost in this state of apparent vacancy, and yet, in these hours of idleness, one learns essential truths about the macrocosm and the microcosm.

***Konrad Lorenz,* King Solomon's Ring**

A zoo is a place where all things must thrive: animals, science, conservation, creativity, discovery. It seems only natural, therefore, that a zoo should be primarily a place for learning. Of our fundamental objectives—conservation, education, science, and recreation—the "straw that stirs the drink" is education. Our community certainly values education above all other virtues of the zoo, and it is something we focused on very closely as we rebuilt Zoo Atlanta. Education is what we do best.

At our zoo, education is not restricted to formal classroom programs, although we do offer such programs—lectures and all—for virtually every age group and for teachers. The zoo's best teachers have four legs, long sticky tongues, hooves, and horns. They are big and they are small, and by living their lives they teach us about life itself. Our zoo exhibits are chock full of education and entertainment, what some people have dubbed "edu-tainment." We engage the visitor in many ways, to help the animals tell their story. Through compelling and colorful graphics, we supply passive, but hopefully fascinating, details about the animals. Our interpretive naturalists (some are called "docents") provide information in a friendly, more active manner. We have found that zoo education works best when human beings exchange ideas about the events they have just witnessed. Our visitors enjoy their interactions with our "experts-in-residence," and they especially appreciate insider information about a recent birth, or the latest news about Willie B.'s love life.

All of our professional staff and every one of our volunteers are, first and foremost, zoo educators. We also use trained volunteers in our animal shows and in special programs like the Zoomobile, where animals accompany their caretakers to schools, hospitals, and day care centers. In an interview conducted by Erika Archibald and published in *Atlanta Magazine* (1988), Jon Coe discussed the meaning of "greatness" when applied to zoo education:

> The criteria for a great zoo, says Coe, start with what the zoo stands for, what its message is, what people take home with them and what they remember five years later. "In the best case, visitors who came for a good time leave having learned a lot without even knowing they were taught."

The zoo is our primary venue for education, but we especially enjoy those occasions when we can take our most loyal supporters on safari. Several times each year, zoo staff accompany zoo enthusiasts on voyages to distant lands to see wildlife in its natural habitats. Zoo tour groups have recently been to Kenya, Tanzania, Indonesia, Australia, the Galapagos Islands, and coastal Mexico. In such places, we continue to teach about the fragility of our natural world. And, by educating others, we continue our own education about the ecosystems that we are desperately trying to save. Travel is one of the all-time great perks for zoo men and women. We enjoy it, and our careers are enriched by it. Zoo supporters are drawn much closer to the cause when they explore wildlife with the help of knowledgeable zoo staff.

At the zoo, we have tried to make even our formal educa-

A barn owl gets set to fly during Zoo Atlanta's "Travelling Talons" educational program. (Photograph by Steve Rasé)

tion programs unusual, and lots of fun. Picture this: Dusk is falling. All the visitors have gone home, and the only sounds in the zoo now are from the animals—donkeys braying, sea lions barking, peacocks calling. Soon it's completely dark. Suddenly, out of nowhere, a bunch of jiggling, twinkling, moving little lights appear. Slowly, they slide up the hill and disappear into the trees. Hushed voices can be heard, traveling on a cool breeze: "ooh," "aah," "sshh." No, it's not a bunch of bandits. It's the "Nightcrawlers," folks from one of our educational programs. In addition to the exciting night hike, Nightcrawlers get to learn all about how the zoo operates behind the scenes. They see everything from the zoo's kitchen, where the animals' diets are prepared, to the greenhouses, where tropical plants and trees are grown. They play special animal games, see wildlife films, and enjoy hands-on experiences with snakes, ferrets, and alligators. Then they pull out their sleeping bags and spend the night in our education center. In the morning, there are more activities before the experience is over. And the program is not limited to just kids. Any group of any age is welcome.

For those who don't want to brave the overnight experience, we have lots of other group programs for kids. Project Discovery, for example, can be tailored to the desires of any group, whether it be for up-close experiences with animals or learning about careers at zoos. During the summer, kids attend day camp at the zoo, for a week of fun, hands-on experiences. We have programs for adults, too, ranging from lectures by renowned conservationists, such as Richard Leakey and Jane Goodall, to intensive training to become one of our volunteer naturalists.

In fact, becoming a volunteer at the zoo is one of the best education experiences of all, with the opportunity to learn directly from our dedicated animal experts. Keepers, curators, and other zoo specialists really know their critters, and volunteers are in the best position to learn from them. Other experts also pass through, to visit our renowned zoo or to give informal talks to the staff, and volunteers and other dedicated members are encouraged to join in. This is just one more way to get close to the world of animals and conservation, and it can be almost as thrilling as getting to know the critters themselves. Some of my own biggest thrills have come in this way, such as when I had lunch with the great naturalist George Schaller in the staff dining room at the Bronx Zoo in 1981. A few years later, I was invited to a picnic with Jane Goodall and North Carolina Zoo director Bob Fry. We picnicked in a tiny park in Greensboro and had a great time talking about chimpanzees. Close encounters like these are available to our staff and supporters as well, through functions at the zoo, and in other ways. For example, Zoo Atlanta staff have been interested in the work of Cynthia Moss, an expert on the behavior of African elephants, and we have contributed funds to support her two African student assistants at Amboseli Park in Kenya, where she has worked for more than a decade. One of our most dedicated volunteers, Wayne Esarove, actually arranged for an Isuzu truck to be donated to the project. It was desperately needed. In turn, Moss has twice visited with our supporters in Atlanta, and we have taken some of them to Kenya to visit her in Amboseli. On those occasions we had the unforgettable experience of living in the bush and studying wild elephants.

While we zoo people often travel to the wild to learn, we also try, along with other conservation organizations, to lend a hand toward wildlife education in other countries. Sometimes that involves working with local people to help them protect their valuable and important natural resources. In Kenya, for example, local people, organized into Wildlife Clubs, convinced their national government to ban trade in wildlife products. These Wildlife Clubs were founded and nurtured by representatives of the African Wildlife Foundation, who have also assisted in developing educational programs in Rwanda, encouraging local people to protect their national parks and respect the gorillas and other wildlife living in their midst. For wild places to survive, local people must value them and receive some tangible benefits for their efforts in protection.

Zoos are increasingly getting involved in such projects to stimulate local preservation efforts. Zoo Atlanta has been working to assist the tiny Belize Zoo, to help the local people appreciate the wild animals around them. We feel that if we can influence public opinion there, the wild animals will be safer. While traveling through Ecuador recently, on the way to the Galapagos Islands, I was advised by local tour guides not to visit the local zoo in Quito. I greeted this advice with great sadness. The zoo was turning off the tourists and surely was not benefitting the local people, either. These zoos should be "windows" into the wild, preparing visitors for adventures ahead and providing local people with greater appreciation and understanding of their native wildlife. We feel that by helping to save and improve these little zoos, we are recruiting partnerships to help save rain forests. The Quito Zoo, like so many others, needs a strong partner to help it serve the local people.

Black rhinos Boma and Rosetta are both very friendly under the appropriate conditions and are fond of apples and carrots.
(Photograph by Terry L. Maple)

Many zoos are forming "Sister Zoo" partnerships with small zoos in developing countries, in order to help advance standards at such zoos. For example, a group of American zoos (the Zoo Conservation Outreach Group) is working with zoos in Central and South America, sponsoring programs and providing equipment and supplies. Zoo Atlanta, in partnership with the New York Zoological Society, is attempting to revitalize the dilapidated Entebbe Zoo in Uganda.

Early in my university career, I discovered that zoos were like living laboratories, teaching anything from basic skills to detailed specialties. For example, in a zoo you can find nearly every type of social organization, locomotion, sensory specialization, and cognitive style, making it a boon for teachers of biology and psychology. I first used Atlanta's zoo as a teaching resource for undergraduate students in psychology, finding it perfect for the basic course in animal behavior. The students could easily observe a multitude of animals and gather data for term papers. Advanced students could be plugged into ongoing research projects.

For many years, I have used the zoo as a lab for my Georgia Tech undergraduate course in environmental psychology. Each fall I teach this course with Dr. Jean Wineman of the College of Architecture and we assign our students to design exhibits for animals. This work requires them to interview zoo staff, do background reading, spend long hours in the zoo, and occasionally visit nearby zoos for different perspectives. These students never fail to come up with bizarre and wonderful ideas. One student reacted to the challenge of designing a manatee exhibit by arranging to scuba dive in their midst. He brought back a videotape of his encounter to illustrate his ideas. We also use our consulting architects and some of our zoo staff to provide special insight into the design process and to react to the student projects.

But the scope of zoo education is even greater than this, and we have found that the zoo easily teaches children as young as kindergarten age. So today at the zoo we offer special workshops for teachers, to help them make use of the zoo as a resource. We provide special training and curriculum materials, emphasizing endangered species and rain forests. As a result of these programs, the zoo has been designated as a prime, recommended educational opportunity by Werner Rogers, Georgia's state superintendent of schools. In fact, students who participate in the zoo's educational programs during the school day are considered to be continuing their in-class curriculum.

Perhaps one of our most unique formal programs is the "Young Scientist Program," which combines our strengths in science and education. This program, which was developed by Dr. Beth Stevens, director of our Conservation Action Resource Center, in conjunction with our educational staff, brings gifted middle-school students to the zoo for

Architect Jon Coe confronts fantasy figure Mr. Zuma, who was originally created for cartoon-strip graphics. Mr. Zuma is played here by Terry Richardson. (Photograph by Terry L. Maple)

a special curriculum. Here they learn how to become zoo biologists, observing and recording animal behavior for specific projects that are planned with the assistance of professional zoo staff. They conclude their studies by writing scientific reports based on their findings, and I am always impressed by the high quality of their work.

"Jambo. My name is Mr. Zuma. I'm the warden of a game park in East Africa. My job is to protect the wild animals that live in the park from poachers who illegally hunt and kill animals for their horns, ivory, skins, and meat."

You may feel like you're on safari, but you're actually in Zoo Atlanta's new Masai Mara exhibit. Mr. Zuma is a fictional character who appears on signs throughout this east African plains area. This is another type of education we like to engage in, so that our visitors may learn important concepts about conservation while they have fun experiencing our exhibits. Occasionally, Mr. Zuma even comes alive (with the help of one of our education staff members) and "catches" some poachers loose in the zoo. This really brings the issue to life.

As visitors venture farther into the Masai Mara, they run into some other surprising sights, such as a large elephant skull sticking out of the grass and a giant, pointed mound of red dirt. The awesome (and authentic) elephant skull represents the tragic results of elephant poaching, and a small clipboard sign provides an informal explanation. The mound of dirt is our re-creation of the giant termite mounds that dot the landscape in east Africa.

Nearby, visitors may run into a khaki-clad person, whom we call a docent, with a small cart. On this cart may be an elephant tusk, a rhino horn, and varied artifacts made from the skins, hides, and teeth of endangered animals, all confiscated by the U.S. Fish and Wildlife Service and loaned to us for public education. This specially

These pants would fit an adult male gorilla, as Deputy Zoo Director Jeff Swanagan explains. The zoo tries to educate children in fun ways.
(Photograph by Joe Sebo)

trained volunteer is a fountain of information about the animals, the exhibits, and conservation issues. How did the poachers get the elephant tusk? Why do poachers kill rhinos? Where exactly are the Serengeti Plains of Africa? The docents can discuss answers to these difficult questions. They also handle many small, tame animals, such as hedgehogs, snakes, tortoises, and ferrets, introducing them to our visitors to carefully touch and examine up close.

Another fun way we teach visitors about wildlife is through specialized animal shows. At our daily elephant show, visitors witness the elephant's incredible strength and dexterity, and they learn about the plight of this species in the wild. At the end of the show, the elephant holds up a sign that reads, "Don't buy ivory." Next door, in our wildlife theater, "NatureQuest" is a live dramatic presentation featuring humans and animals confronting various conservation dilemmas. These interactive programs help make our new zoo worlds apart from the old one.

For those who can't make it to the zoo or who want a little preview, the Zoomobile can bring the zoo to them. The Zoomobile consists of a special group of staff, volunteers, and animals who travel around the region, putting on special presentations for schools and other groups. Sometimes our animals travel with a unique five-piece wind ensemble, presenting a special program called "ZooMusic."

Learning at the zoo is fun, and in our special programs we impart plenty of useful information. But our goal goes way beyond fun and teaching. What we are really trying to do is help people make emotional connections with the animals. Baba Diom of Senegal elegantly expressed this idea: "In the end, we will conserve only what we love . . . we will love only what we know . . . and we will know only what we are taught." That explains beautifully what we try to do at the zoo.

We at the zoo have come to recognize no greater commitment than providing opportunities for people to know the animals as we have come to know them. Indeed, the success of our programs is noteworthy: more than 178,000 children came to the zoo on school-sponsored visits in 1991, for instance. But we also have lots of additional, creative education ideas that we cannot yet afford, and there are many we wish to expand. Hopefully an endowment for our new Conservation Action Resource Center, under which our education department now operates, will help us bring even more of these ideas to life.

One of the most important tasks of any zoo is to help those who enroll in our education programs to become more science literate. Science literacy is becoming an important national issue, and zoo education clearly contributes to its development. It is something we are now working hard to promote. One can see how zoos fit into science literacy by the definition James Rutherford and Andrew Ahlgren offer in their recent book *Science for All Americans* (1989):

> . . . the scientifically literate person is one who is aware that science, mathematics, and technology are interdependent human enterprises with strengths and limitations; understands key concepts and principles of science; is familiar with the natural world and recognizes both its diversity and unity; and uses scientific knowledge and scientific ways of thinking for individual and social purposes.

One way to advance science literacy is to encourage interaction between children and scientists. We have recruited highly skilled zoo biologists and designed programs so that these individuals are accessible to students in the public school systems. One method we plan to use is called "distance learning" technology. These are systems whereby kids at distant locations can receive live telecasts from the zoo or from a zoo field station. Soon, students in Albany, Georgia, will be able to talk directly to our staff in Atlanta, or better yet, in the Okefenokee Swamp, where we will provide information and a close-up look at Georgia wildlife. My first experience with this technology came in 1990 in San Antonio, when Jack Hanna, director of the Columbus Zoo in Ohio, and I participated in the first live call-in show broadcast from Sea World. People from all over the country were connected to us through cable networks and asked us an array of questions about zoos and aquariums. The Sea World parks have since led the way in developing this kind of educational technology.

One of the most remarkable examples of technology and education working together is a program called "Live from Monterey Canyon," produced by the Monterey Bay Aquarium. Scientists from the aquarium conduct their studies of the nearby submarine canyon in full view of the public via a "remotely operated vehicle." This submersible vehicle sends back images, and an interpreter answers questions and describes the action as it occurs. The interpreter and the audience can communicate directly with staff on the mother ship, and can use a computerized encyclopedia to get additional video, photographs, and notes about the many fascinating creatures who inhabit the canyon.

At the Dallas Zoo, educators are advancing science literacy with a program called "ImagineAfrica," which uses their new "Wilds of Africa" exhibit. In this program, sixth-grade students assume the roles of field biologists working in East Africa, using the exhibit as their "game reserve." Over the course of five weeks, they study six major habitats and learn to use cameras and binoculars and to keep field journals. After data have been gathered and analyzed, the students are encouraged to make recommendations for resolving various ecological dilemmas in the "Wilds of Africa." In this way, the students are even helping solve real-world problems, in addition to learning about science. As zoo exhibits become increasingly naturalistic, they will be far more useful to our school systems. As we rebuilt Zoo Atlanta, we found that naturalistic zoo habitats are good for the animals, great for research, and excellent sites for education.

GREAT APES AND EXPECTATIONS

If your company is serious about quality improvements, you must ultimately strive for perfection. . . . A big danger is not setting your goal high enough.

Donald E. Petersen, **A Better Idea**

In 1986, I received a visit from James Donaldson, marketing czar for the Ford Motor Company. My confidants referred to him as "Diamond Jim." He was a Scot who still spoke with a bit of a brogue, and he was full of confidence and wit. My assignment was to show him the zoo and then receive a check for $100,000. It was my kind of day.

Unfortunately, the zoo was pretty grim in those days. We had cleaned and painted the place, and the landscaping was beginning to work its magic, but it was still a long way from the naturalistic showcase that it would become in a few years. Still, I could paint a persuasive picture of the future, and I talked at length about our plans for gorillas. Donaldson seemed pleased when I told him that we were going to build "the very best gorilla exhibit in the world." Later that morning, as we awaited our turn at the podium, he whispered to me: "When we give you all the money, Terry, your gorilla exhibit had better not be number two!" His challenge caught me by surprise, and we had a good chuckle, but I refused to be intimidated. The fire of competition was in me, too, and I was proud to be associated with a corporation whose motto was: "Quality is job one." I knew at once that we would be compatible partners in the rebuilding of Zoo

Atlanta. "You don't have to be the biggest to be the best," Donaldson reminded me. Given the significance of their support, I was very pleased when in 1988 the *Atlanta Journal and Constitution* opined:

> Not all zoos can boast an angel among their critters, but Zoo Atlanta can, and all of Atlanta is better off because of it. The angel is the Ford Motor Co. What Ford has done for the zoo, and is continuing to do, is remarkable.

Zoo Atlanta is, indeed, modest in size, but we have big plans, big ideas, and a pretty big reputation for the quality of our work. At 37.5 acres, we aim to be "the best 40-acre zoo in the world." We can never have the largest animal collection (the San Diego Zoo has more than 5,000 animals, while we have about 1,000), nor the greatest acreage (the North Carolina Zoo has 1,148 acres), but we have designed and built some of the highest-quality exhibitry in the world.

FIVE GREAT ZOOS ON MODEST ACREAGE

(Less Than 60 Acres)

1. Audubon Zoo, New Orleans	58 acres
2. Lincoln Park Zoo, Chicago	35 acres
3. **Zoo Atlanta**, Georgia	37 acres
4. Toledo Zoo, Ohio	51 acres
5. Philadelphia Zoo, Pennsylvania	42 acres

The Ford African Rainforest, where our gorillas and other animals are housed, is the one exhibit that speaks the most about our intentions. It is composed of five outdoor habitats, the largest of which is more than 27,000 square feet. In the two largest of these enclosures, hundred-year-old hardwood trees reside majestically alongside newly planted vegetation provided for shade and consumption. (Our gorillas consumed more than $20,000 of vegetation in their first month on exhibit, so our horticulturists have an ongoing battle on their hands. As in the wild, our gorillas eat themselves out of house and home and we must replace the material that is lost, but we have learned to "feed" them less expensive flora!)

Is our gorilla exhibit the best? Since I am an expert on the subject of gorillas in captivity, I am often asked such questions. It is difficult to say because the exhibits differ in so many ways and there is no standard index by which to judge. For example, the largest collection of gorillas on exhibit in this country is at Lincoln Park in Chicago (21 animals). Zoo Atlanta exhibits the second largest collection, 17 animals (with all but one belonging to the Yerkes Primate Center).

Zoo Atlanta is the only zoo in the world currently exhibiting four families of gorillas, however, and we devote the most space of any American zoo to their exhibition and management. Since our gorillas are arranged in contiguous social groups, as they would live in the wild, I believe that we have achieved the most authentic simulation of true gorilla life. (Our gorillas lack only poachers to make their experience truly real.) So, while I believe we have created the world's best gorilla exhibit, there are many other praiseworthy contenders.

The gorilla exhibit at Woodland Park Zoo in Seattle, which opened in 1977, was clearly the best when I publicly endorsed it in the mid-1980s. The naturalism of this exhibit has never been surpassed, but it houses only one group of gorillas. (Modifications completed in 1992 will permit the exhibition of a second group.) It is the epitome of Robert Sommer's construct "soft architecture." David Hancocks, who helped design the exhibit, explained it this way:

> We considered it essential to create a habitat as close to the real thing as possible. It was our belief that visitors make subconscious links and we intended that they should never again associate gorillas with cages. Instead we wanted to instill images of the great apes amid lush vegetation, climbing trees, lounging among thick shrubbery, living in a green world. Perhaps then, when people heard or

read about habitat destruction, they would understand why gorillas cannot survive without forests.

The innovations of this gorilla exhibit are almost too numerous to list. It was the first to provide a winding visitor trail in the midst of dense vegetation, immersing visitors in the gorillas' realm before they spot the animals in a kind of clearing. This dramatic setting is an example of the zoo as "theater": the landscape sets the mood, and suddenly we discover the apes! This exhibit also pioneered the use of living trees, in spite of warnings from other zoo professionals that they would be ruined by the gorillas. Hancocks said, "I suspected that if the gorillas' attentions were distributed among lots of trees, the foliage would survive quite easily. Our mistake was not including more trees, but we were flying in the face of advice from many zoos." The Woodland Park designers were innovative indoors, too, providing flexible sleeping hammocks in the gorillas' night quarters.

My favorite gorilla exhibit in Europe is in Holland at a small park known as Apenheul. I visited this specialized zoo

Paki and Maki were the first two Atlanta gorillas to give birth in the zoo's long history. (Photograph by Joe Sebo)

in 1979 and was very impressed with it. Apenheul's owner, Wim Mager, devotes his space exclusively to gorillas and selected monkeys. The gorilla habitat is an island surrounded by a water-filled moat and provides a single group of gorillas with more space than any other zoo in the world, at two hectares (nearly five acres). The grassy island contains tall pine trees, which are protected by concrete cylinders. The gorillas' night house includes six interconnecting rooms and offers additional protection during the day in winter.

The gorilla exhibits in Atlanta, Woodland Park, and Apenheul all provide the animals with plenty of space and large social units. Gorillas thrive under these conditions, and the people who visit them are enriched by the experience. Recently many other zoos have begun to build naturalistic gorilla exhibits. My current rankings for overall quality would be as follows:

1. Zoo Atlanta's Ford African Rainforest (built in 1988)
2. Woodland Park Zoo (1977)
3. San Diego Zoo (1991)
4. Busch Gardens (1992)
5. Dallas Zoo (1989)

Many of these newest exhibits take advantage of state-of-the-art technology. For example, San Diego's exhibit features a $250,000 sound system that broadcasts rain forest sounds obtained from a genuine West African gorilla habitat. The system has multiple tracks, 111 speakers, 27 sensors, and random distribution of sound patterns and sequences. Dr. Jackie Ogden, formerly of Zoo Atlanta's research department, evaluated this sound system for her doctoral dissertation at Georgia Tech. She found that visitors reported the sound system made them feel like they really were in a rain forest, and that it increased their awareness of the natural environment. They also reported positive emotional shifts due to the sounds. These results clearly demonstrate that multisensory immersion techniques enhance the visitor's experience. At Zoo Atlanta we are planning a rain forest sound system for use day and night. In our "Nightcrawlers" educational program, trained interpretive naturalists will help the kids to identify the sounds they hear in the dark.

In addition to naturalistic exhibits like ours, there are other successful gorilla collections where the animals are living in older facilities, such as those at the zoos in the Bronx, Cincinnati, Columbus, and Lincoln Park. Each of these zoos is successful in breeding gorillas, with Columbus and Lincoln Park especially well known for their programs of management, husbandry, and science. Columbus was the first zoo to breed gorillas in 1956; it is also unique in having built a replica of the successful "mega-cage" first developed at Howlett's Park in England. To me these giant steel cages are genuinely ugly, but the gorillas seem to like them just fine. They work because they are very large and can be filled with interesting "toys" and climbing structures, but the steel bars obscure our view and remind us that the animals are our captives. Visitors prefer naturalism, but naturalistic enclosures are more expensive to build. This type of enclosure was developed by Howlett's John Aspinall, who suggested the following simple principles of gorilla management:

1. Keep them in large groups.
2. Large indoor playroom and extensive well-equipped outdoor runs with a roof open to weather and cobwebbed with brachiating bars. . . .
3. Deep litter of oat straw in outside run for foraging and day nesting. Straw also for bedding inside house.
4. Numerous outside contraptions for plays: chutes, paddling pools, metal trees, platforms, suspended spheres of galvanized piping, giant marker buoys, a hanging garden of sisal ropes, . . . etc.
5. At least 200 types of food a year. . . .
6. Keepers to be encouraged to stay with the gorillas

all their lives and strengthen bonds with them.

7. Treat gorillas at least as equal or superior to man.

Aspinall is untrained in zoology and makes his living primarily from his casinos. Nevertheless, most of his ideas about gorilla management are sound (although he is controversial for his habit of entering the gorillas' enclosure). In American zoos like the Atlanta Zoo for most of this century, we kept gorillas in isolation or in pairs, confined to small cages and sterile, barren facilities. We provided no variety in food, and often had untrained, punitive caretakers for the animals. Gorillas were routinely subordinated to humans. These technique were wrong, and Aspinall somehow knew it. The management of gorillas in captivity is both art and science. For a very long time, zoos had difficulty just keeping gorillas alive. (No real effort was made to breed them until the early 1950s.)

Gorillas have always been a big draw at the zoo, due to their size, strength, and presumed ferocity. They do look plenty fierce and possess the power to defend themselves against almost any living thing, but they are quite agreeable creatures under normal circumstances. In 1933, Belle Benchley, then director of the San Diego Zoo, commented on the temperament of the zoo's two gorillas, Mbongo and Ngagi:

> Mbongo and Ngagi show none of the ferocity earlier attributed to the gorilla. They are, in fact, exceedingly good-natured toward each other and those of us who do the most with them.

Although they are truly "gentle giants," the sheer size of gorillas can be intimidating, and perhaps that helps explain their popularity. Mbongo reached the incredible weight of 602 pounds, while his cagemate Ngagi weighed in at 539 pounds. These gorillas were thought at the time to be mountain gorillas but now are classified as the Eastern lowland subspecies. Both of these types are slightly larger than the Western lowland gorilla, which is the type we see in zoos today (and which rarely exceeds 500 pounds in captivity). Gorillas are so big that if they wore a coat, it

Willie B. makes the cover! Would you refuse funds to this austere-looking primate? (Photograph by Joe Sebo and courtesy of *Fundraising Management* magazine)

would have to be sewn in size 62, with extra-long arms. Their hands are massive. They are extremely muscular. No one has calculated the exact strength of a gorilla, but they have successfully defeated a dozen men in tug-of-war contests. Dr. Terry Todd at the University of Texas, a worldwide authority on strength, believes that gorillas are the equal of well-trained human power lifters. Imagine what they could do if they trained like people do! When he visited our gorillas in Atlanta, Dr. Todd was amazed at their agility, at how easily they move their huge bodies around their enclosures. If they are as strong as power lifters, they are also as nimble as gymnasts.

A lot of people ask me about Willie B.'s diet. Our nutritionist, Gloria Hamor, working under the direction of our veterinarian, Dr. Rita McManamon, is responsible for the specialized diets of each individual animal. Dr. McManamon tries to keep Willie on a diet that keeps him trim. At one time he weighed more than 500 pounds, but now he weighs in at a svelte 450. Gorillas eat a great variety of foods in the wild, so we try to provide them with a varied diet in the zoo. The following is Willie B.'s typical daily menu:

5 apples
4 oranges
1 1/2 lbs. carrots or sweet potatoes
4/5 lb. cabbage, collards, and/or broccoli
3/4 cup peanuts
3 qt. nonfat milk
1 lb. high-protein monkey chow
3 tbs. raisins

He also receives, seasonally, cuttings of bamboo, banana leaves, willow, sugar cane, etc., and scattered sunflower and other seed mixes inside and outside to encourage active foraging. We try to distribute the food in ways that will encourage activity. Gorillas spend a lot of time foraging in the wild (up to 40 percent of a day), so we must do what we can to keep them busier in the zoo. If we fail to keep them active, they are prone to coprophabia (consumption of feces) and regurgitation/reingestion. These behaviors endanger the gorillas' health and upset zoo visitors.

How long do these great creatures live? Most of what we know about gorilla longevity comes from the Philadelphia Zoo's Massa, who lived to be about fifty-four years old. His exact age is not known, since he was captured in the wild. I was a guest at his fiftieth birthday party and had a chance to study him more closely. At fifty, he was very thin and walked cautiously. Most of his teeth had been pulled. His body was silvery and his hair sparse, contributing even further to his aged appearance. He really looked older than fifty, which seems to be the upper bound of the gorilla's lifespan. Dian Fossey believed that mountain gorillas lived into their sixties in the wild, but she could produce no evidence to support this claim. At the Philadelphia Zoo, Massa benefitted from an acclaimed nutritional regimen. However, he lived most of his life alone, and whether that has any effect on lifespan is unknown.

People often ask me how long we expect Willie B. to live. Since he is now about thirty-five and in very good health, he may be a candidate for a new longevity record. As the new patriarch of a five-animal harem, his additional responsibilities may provide him extra will to live, or the stress of social living may have more negative effects. One thing is certain: He is much more active now that he is living outside with other animals. He has lost excess weight and has gained muscle tone. Overall, he is a healthier gorilla.

A CHRONOLOGY OF THE LIFE OF WILLIE B.

1961 – Willie B. arrives at the Atlanta Zoo.
1980 – His fame grows as a television watcher.
1981 – Maple and Coe develop a concept for Willie's future habitat.

1984 – Yerkes agrees to loan other gorillas to the zoo.
1985 – Ford commits resources to build the world's best gorilla exhibit.
1988 – Willie moves into the outside exhibit in the Ford African Rainforest.
1989 – Yerkes females Kinyani and Katoomba successfully socialize Willie.
1989 – Willie B. copulates with Kinyani.
1992 – Two mature females are added; he copulates with Choomba; the group is moved to the largest habitat (17,000 square feet).

The average zoo-goer (and primatologist) sooner or later begins to speculate about the intelligence of gorillas. Turn-of-the-century naturalists, such as Albert Ernest Jenks, were more impressed with the gorilla's strength than intellect, as can be seen in this passage from his paper "Bulu Knowledge of the Gorilla and Chimpanzee," published in 1911.

> The native rates the gorilla as superior to most of the other animals of Kamerun [*sic*], though he wins this distinction more because of his prowess as a fighter than because of his exceptional sagacity.

By comparison, the naturalist R. L. Garner depicted the gorilla in a slightly different light. In the following passage from *Gorillas and Chimpanzees* (1896), he also applied lore from field experiences to speculate about the animal's intellectual powers:

> The intellect of the gorilla must not be under-rated. He studies the motives and intentions of man with a keen perception, and is seldom mistaken in his interpretation of them.

In our 1982 book *Gorilla Behavior*, Mike Hoff and I

reviewed what was known about the mind of the gorilla, and we concluded that the animal was the intellectual equal of the chimpanzee or the orangutan. In captivity, at least, the gorilla learns just as readily as do the other ape taxa. However, unlike their anthropoid cousins, gorillas have not yet been observed to fashion "tools" in the wild. The absence of such behavior is a bit of a mystery. Perhaps gorillas' resources are so abundant, and their motive to feed so focused, that they simply don't "need" to use tools.

In the zoo, we see clear evidence of species differences among the apes. Their "intelligence" is certainly manifested in different ways, and they are temperamentally quite different. The gorilla is quiet and indifferent, the orangutan is methodical and curious, the chimpanzee is noisy, active, and charismatic. Can you imagine the efficiency of an ape with the size and strength of the gorilla, the tenacity and ingenuity of the orangutan, and the temperament of the volatile chimpanzee? Such a creature would be a formidable competitor for humankind.

When you discuss the intelligence of apes, it is impossible to avoid the ape language controversy. Two gorillas at the Gorilla Foundation in Woodside, California, have learned to interact with people using the American Sign Language system. Koko, the most advanced of the anthropoid students, is said to use more than 300 signs. A number of chimpanzees have also learned this and other systems of symbolic interaction, and Koko appears to be their intellectual peer. There is no question that Koko is "communicating" when she signs. But it is difficult to demonstrate that her signing is the equivalent of human communication. Since Koko's training situation has not been replicated elsewhere, it would be hazardous to accept all of the claims that have been made about her abilities. Her musings on the afterlife, for instance, have been suggested without a hint of healthy skepticism. Koko's activities have become so "personalized," and so heavily marketed, that it is difficult to separate the science from the hyperbole. Koko's high public profile has created demand for ever more incredible findings. It is, in fact, quite difficult to be wholly objective when a project is dependent on the generosity of public donors. Zoo professionals understand this problem, since many of our animals are also public, media figures. It just means that science has to be autonomous and separate from marketing efforts.

While I have some reservations about the interpretations of Koko's accomplishments, I am delighted with her contributions as an ambassador for gorillakind. If people value gorillas more because of Koko, and I think they do, then she is contributing to our stewardship of gorillas in captivity and in the wild. This is exactly how we hope Willie B. functions, symbolically speaking. As conservation, Koko's message works very well, and we should be grateful for the difference she is making. Recently, the gorilla management committee for AAZPA's Species Survival Plan (SSP) approved the loan of an adult male gorilla to the Gorilla Foundation in an attempt to breed Koko. In order to receive this male, from the Cincinnati Zoo, the Gorilla Foundation had to agree to abide by SSP regulations. This includes objective decision making about the disposition of any future offspring. The committee could decide, for example, that Koko's offspring should return to a zoo colony to grow up in a group, among peers. We hope that Koko will mate successfully and demonstrate appropriate maternal behavior. We may ultimately learn something about the experience of gorilla parenting if she decides to sign about it. Of course, we would have to interpret her "utterances" with great care and parsimony.

Other organizations are doing tremendous work to help save gorillas and other apes, and we at zoos both participate in and learn from such work. I am privileged to serve on the board of directors for one such group, the Dian Fossey Gorilla Fund (DFGF, previously known as the Digit Fund). This non-profit corporation is responsible for the stewardship of the Karisoke Research Center, founded by Fossey in Rwanda's Parc des Volcans, and her records, memorabilia, and personal effects. Although founded by Fossey herself, this fund was successfully nurtured by Ruth Keesling and a small cadre of dedicated conservationists. The board of directors, seeking to strengthen its mission, recently hired a professional executive, Richard Block. (Block was once curator of education at Zoo Atlanta and has also served as director of public programs at the World Wildlife Fund.) Since only about 600 mountain gorillas still exist in Africa, DFGF has an awesome responsibility. It is the only site dedicated solely to studying and saving this species. DFGF's conservation activities include antipoaching patrols who monitor the park daily, remove snares and traps, and collect information about the gorillas' health and location. Karisoke is also a center for education for people of all ages in Rwanda and beyond. AAZPA's SSP committee for gorillas is working to generate financial support for Karisoke, which, like many field conservation projects, needs institutional partners to provide financial and human resources. Just a few thousand dollars can outfit park rangers with protective gear, or extend the life of a vehicle for another year. Volunteers can help rebuild housing, and educators can improve park signage or write tourist guidebooks.

My own connection with Dian Fossey stems from my role in recruiting a student research assistant for Karisoke back in 1979. I had been contacted by my friend Dr. Ramon Rhine, who was at that time a member of the Karisoke research advisory board and was looking for young talent to work in Rwanda. I had just returned from my month-long course "Field Work in Animal Behavior" and had supervised several undergraduates who seemed worthy of the assignment. John Fowler, the outstanding bird watcher of the group (who joined us later at Zoo Atlanta), was my first choice. Fowler seemed eager for the chance to spend a year watching wild gorillas and was off to Rwanda within a few months. The actual date—January 8, 1990—is one I can't forget, since it is also the birthday of Alfred Russel Wallace, a contemporary of Darwin and cofounder of the theory of natural selection. We at the zoo celebrate both birthdays regularly, but Wallace's is our favorite. Fowler went off to Africa with a specially "decomposed" song, sung to the tune of "Alfie." I offer herein just a few bars of this, admittedly, insider lyric:

What's it all about, Alfred?
Is it just for lust that we live?
What's it all about
When you lose your snout, Alfred?
Are we meant to be more than apekind,
or are we all one kind? . . .
I believe in mind, Alfred.
Without the mind we just exist, Alfred.
Until you find the mind you've missed, you're nothing, Alfred.
When he walks let his knuckles lead the way;
he'll evolve any day, Alfred.

Fowler had good reason to sing this song in Africa, since it was useful comic relief from the otherwise arduous experience. Fossey came to value his work, and he was one of the few human beings she mentioned by name in her book, *Gorillas in the Mist*. Fowler's insights gave me a greater understanding of the situation at Karisoke, and of Dian Fossey's temperament. At the time, she was in a great deal of trouble with the Rwandan authorities, due to her fierce antipoaching activities, or her "active conservation," as she labeled it. Fossey had been devastated by the brutal decapitation of her beloved gorilla Digit, and pursued poachers with a vengeance. She left the camp in 1981, in the midst of the controversy, however, and spent two years at Cornell University writing her book.

It just so happened that I was writing my book *Gorilla*

Behavior at the same time. My publishers sent Dian Fossey an advance copy of the book as soon as it was available, and she reviewed it for *Animal Kingdom*, the magazine of the New York Zoological Society. Unfortunately, she didn't seem to like the book and especially took issue with those sections dealing with gorillas in the wild. Apparently, we were encroaching on her scientific turf, and my recent examination of her personal copy of the book, replete with penciled commentary in the margins, confirms it. Wherever we quoted other scientists who had worked at Karisoke, Fossey wrote in expletives and other disdainful comments. Next to some citations of other Karisoke field biologists, she wrote boldly, "my data!" Apparently the gorilla business can be as competitive as any! Luckily, other reviews of my book were favorable, so I feel confident that Fossey's response was an aberration. It wasn't personal, either, since we got along quite well whenever we met at conferences and the like. I have come to understand her feelings at that difficult time in her life. All students of gorillas are really on the same side, and I feel all of our work can help animals both in zoos and in the wild.

As an observer of gorillas, a consultant on their behavior and zoo management, and a zoo director, I have been fortunate to come to know many gorillas (even beyond the many in our zoo) and to be in the position of helping numerous others. In many cases, questions come by telephone from curators who don't want to make a risky move without some advice. Of the many questions we have received, the most ubiquitous one has concerned the removal of infant gorillas from their mothers. Zoo professionals have agonized about this for years, torn between the need to give new mothers experience and the fear of losing an infant due to possible neglect by the mother. This kind of advice is very difficult to give by phone, and that is one reason I wrote *Gorilla Behavior* (and *Orangutan Behavior*). Careful scientific descriptions of gorilla parenting, for example, can provide curators and keepers with knowledge about the norms, helping them to make good decisions. Videotapes are even better, such as those made by Jörg Hess at the Basel Zoo, documenting gorilla social behavior in exhaustive detail.

Of all of the cases of gorilla behavior that I have been involved in, two stories stand out. The first is the story of Timmy, who was selected by the gorilla SSP committee to be moved for breeding from the Cleveland Zoo to the Bronx Zoo. This plan was greeted by loud objections from animal rights advocates. They argued that Timmy was happy in Cleveland, in his monogamous relationship with a female named Kate, even though Kate was sterile and could not produce offspring. They felt that the Cleveland Zoo was favoring genes over individuals in moving Timmy. The disagreement was sustained for many months by media coverage. Eventually it reached litigation.

About midway through this posturing and bickering, I participated in a conference call, arranged by the lawyers, with the parties involved in the dispute and various "experts." I represented the SSP committee and spoke as an expert on gorilla behavior and management. The "animal rights" side provided a field biologist who had studied mountain gorillas (and had once favorably reviewed my book on gorilla behavior) and an expert on chimpanzee behavior. We argued at length about the importance of moving Timmy, the logistics of the move, and the possible effects on the two gorillas. In the end, the experts agreed only to disagree and the case went to court, where it failed. Timmy was moved to the Bronx Zoo, without further incident. This gorilla who was previously branded as a social failure now has a relationship with a harem of females, and one of his mates just recently became pregnant.

Back in Cleveland, Kate was paired with another male, named Oscar, but that relationship hasn't gone as well. However, since this pair has now moved into a new state-of-the-art tropical house, their lives should improve dramatically. Grouping gorillas is part science, part art, and never easy. Gorillas are moved for many reasons, but the main one is to facilitate breeding, on behalf of all gorillakind. The fate of individual gorillas is always seriously considered. I envision further debates down the road between animal welfare advocates and zoo experts. We will be ready for them.

A better example of how this interaction can succeed can be seen in the case of a gorilla named Ivan. Ivan has lived for twenty years in a glass cage at the B & I department store in western Washington. He lives alone, a curiosity gawked at by curious passersby and sometimes tormenters. His sad plight was featured in Allison Argo's 1991 film *Urban Gorilla*, which was televised as a National Geographic Special. After the film aired, local Washington critics stepped up the pressure on Ivan's owners to do something. A combined effort by PAWS (the Progressive Animal Welfare Society) and concerned zoo directors from the Seattle, Point Defiance, and Dallas zoos has produced better alternatives for Ivan. Zoo Atlanta also offered to board and socialize Ivan. Unfortunately, Ivan remains caged alone at B & I. While the efforts have not yet succeeded, this partnership among zoos and humane groups shows that we can be allies and work together toward the welfare of wildlife.

Like Willie B. before him, Ivan will someday be introduced to a naturalistic habitat, and to other gorillas. When that day comes, it will happen because zoo people and concerned local citizens spoke loud and clear, as they did in Atlanta in 1984.

THE ONCE AND FUTURE ZOO

Except at the zoo, the opportunities to know or even to become interested in wild creatures are largely vicarious for most city dwellers. Yet, the opinions of these urbanites may ultimately shape the future policies of conservation in this country. Seen in this light, the educational challenges to the zoo naturalist and the conservationist are identical.

***William G. Conway,* Science**

Zoo Atlanta celebrated its centennial in 1989. Yet because of a humble beginning and a protracted development, our history had produced very little to brag about. So we chose not to celebrate our past when we reached 100. I had regrets about this, because the National Zoo, which was founded in the same year as the Atlanta Zoo, organized such a creative, enlightened look at its history. But we were able to come up with something almost as satisfying. We decided to look forward, rather than backward. We celebrated our future.

I thought about all the different ways we could characterize a future for our zoo, and, with the help of Clare Richardson, then director of the Friends of Zoo Atlanta, we concocted a phrase that seemed to capture the spirit of our vision: "Conservation Leadership for Our Second Century." It was an ambitious slogan, suggesting, as it did, that we had a big job to do. It also indicated that we regarded our zoo as equal to the task. With our outstanding staff, and an ambitious local community, we felt it was a natural way to envision our future position—seated at the conservation table with the world's great zoos—National, Bronx, San Diego, Brookfield, London, Frankfurt—all larger, wealthier institutions with long histories of involvement in conservation. We celebrated, therefore, our conservation potential.

The formal definition of the word "zoo" doesn't begin to describe the full range of the modern zoo mission. According to the *Oxford American Dictionary*, for example, "zoo" is defined as "a place where wild animals are kept for exhibition and study." Actually this definition is more enlightened than most, as it includes the "study" of wildlife. Many dictionaries also provide a secondary, more troublesome definition. In the *Random House Dictionary*, for example, the secondary definition of "zoo" is "a place, activity, or group marked by chaos or unrestrained behavior." This informal definition is ubiquitous in American life, where people exclaim in their workplace with great frequency, "This place is a zoo!"

This propensity is one reason why officials of the New York Zoological Park (also known as the Bronx Zoo) recently decided to change their name to the International Wildlife Conservation Park. The other zoos under the direction of the 98-year-old New York Zoological Society (hereafter to be known as NYZS/The Wildlife Conservation Society) will use the appellation Wildlife Conservation Center in place of "zoo." These include the facilities at Central Park, Queens, and Prospect Park in Brooklyn. Even the New York Aquarium will be renamed the Aquarium for Wildlife Conservation.

William G. Conway, president of the Wildlife Conservation Society, told the *New York Times* that it was time to recognize the role of the society in its management of 158 conservation and research projects conducted in 41 nations throughout the world. Given the influence of NYZS, many other zoos probably will follow its lead. But for some, including Zoo Atlanta, the problem will not be addressed by a name change, but by changing the meaning of "zoo." If we continue to engage seriously in science, education, and conservation activities, the zoo will become a different kind of enterprise. We must continue to promote our conservation activities and educate our public to understand this shift of emphasis.

One thing is certain. If we are to be successful in our conservation, science, and education mission, we must not abandon our commitment to recreation. The zoo's proper position is "teaching with a smile on our face." Our conservation stories must give our patrons hope and provide opportunities to contribute to projects and programs that can be successful. We can do this because the zoo itself is an example of success. Our living collection is an inspiration to those who would help us to save the wild, and in this way the animals are truly ambassadors for their own kind. The reason that I am comfortable with the word "zoo" in our name is my belief that "zoo" is synonymous with "fun." Because of this, kids do not fall asleep in our classrooms. Learning will always be fun at Zoo Atlanta.

However we choose to label our institutions, all zoos have one common attribute: we exhibit, for the public good, a multitude of living creatures, and they are exhibited under conditions in which they are easily observed and appreciated by millions of people every day. In his most recent draft of the "World Zoo Conservation Strategy," Leobert de Boer emphasized the uniqueness of zoos:

> The fact that all zoos exhibit living specimens of wild animal species underscores the difference between zoos and museums or other cultural and recreational institutions, and is what gives zoos their own unique character.

Clearly, conservation will play a major role in the future of all zoos, as it will at Zoo Atlanta. It is one of the primary goals that has emerged from the soul searching of the zoological community over the past twenty-five years. Consider a recent brochure issued by AAZPA:

> 1. People can read about animals, or see them in films, but nothing replaces the living breathing creature; 2. Animals living in comfortable homes in zoos and aquariums serve as ambassadors to remind us that we must save some wild places, or lose the rich wildlife heritage of the world; 3. Animals such as the Asiatic wild horse, Pere David's deer and the Hawaiian goose would be extinct today if there were no breeding programs.

These statements reflect the recreational, educational, and conservation missions of the modern zoo. And, clearly, the additional area of science supports this tripartite mission.

But no mission is easily, completely, or perfectly completed, and the zoo world has endured its share of critics. Dr. Dale Jamieson, professor of philosophy at the University of Colorado, recently argued that zoos generally do not live up to their own goals. He suggested that zoo animals are deprived of freedom for minimal scientific or public good, that zoos cause suffering and other ills without producing compensatory benefits to animals or humans. James Rachels, writing in the 1976 book *Animal Rights and Human Obligations* (eds. Regan and Singer), submitted another scathing critique:

> It is a familiar fact that many wild animals do not fare at all well in captivity; taken from their natural habitats and put in zoos, they are at first frantic and frustrated because they cannot carry on their normal activities; then they become listless and inactive, shadows of their former selves. Some become vicious and destructive. They often will not reproduce in captivity, and when they do, their young often cannot survive; and finally, members of many species will die sooner in captivity than they would in their natural homes.

These charges certainly applied to the Atlanta Zoo in 1984. The zoo had no clear goals and really was of no benefit to the animals or the visitors. Today, there are still too many zoos adrift in mediocrity, and far too many fall short of

AAZPA's high standards. However, there are also very strong and encouraging trends in the zoo and aquarium profession. For many zoos, the path toward excellence is clear and compelling. But the process of change is extremely costly and time consuming. It took ten years and millions of dollars for the Audubon Zoo to move from being a terrible prison for its animals to being the world-class zoo that it is today. At Zoo Atlanta, we've been rebuilding for eight years, and still one-third of the zoo has not yet been naturalized. As for the largest zoos, it will take many decades to complete their transformation.

However, it is still worthwhile to take our critics very seriously, to examine whether we are progressing satisfactorily toward our goals, to ask whether we really are making a difference in the world. Dr. David Chiszar, a comparative psychologist at the University of Colorado, addressed these questions in his 1985 response to Jamieson, published in *Psychological Record.* In terms of our goal of providing recreation for the public, he concluded that zoos are doing quite well, since three to four hundred million people visit zoos and aquariums each year. In terms of education, zoos have traditionally been well connected with public schools, and many have developed special educational programs and educational components to their exhibits. As for conservation, zoos have developed cooperative species survival plans for the propagation of threatened and endangered species, and they have actually saved some species from extinction (the American bison and the California condor, most notably).

Another very promising conservation development in the zoo world and one in which Zoo Atlanta participates is the emerging Captive Breeding Specialists Group (CBSG). Organized by the Species Survival Commission of the International Union for the Conservation of Nature, the CBSG is a global network of more than 450 volunteer experts from zoos, wildlife agencies, and universities from more than 70 countries. Their mission is to "assist the conservation and establishment of viable populations of threatened species through captive propagation programs and through intensive protection and management of small and fragmented populations in the wild." Says Dr. Ulysses S. Seal, CBSG chairman: "CBSG serves to catalyze cooperation and link programs between the wildlife and captive conservation communities worldwide." A recent meeting to assess the viability of the population and habitat of Sumatran orangutans is an example of this process. In this meeting, CBSG experts provided information and discussed the status of orangutans in Sumatra with Indonesian and other collaborators who will develop a conservation plan to protect the animals. Zoo Atlanta is helping this project by maintaining the zoo world's database for this species.

Zoo Atlanta, like most zoos, also attempts to reflect an ecological consciousness and advocacy in its exhibitry and education programs. We also often work with conservation groups, government agencies, and other institutions to promote environmental awareness. For example, at Zoo Atlanta, we developed a composting exhibit, in conjunction with the local Clean City Commission. In another example, the Denver Zoo, working with the U.S. Fish and Wildlife Service, created a "dead hardwood" exhibit. They demonstrated how a dead hardwood tree is used year after year as a habitat for many types of birds and tree-dwelling creatures. The dead hardwood in the exhibit has a habitat within it and promotes an understanding of how much better it is to leave the dead tree standing, rather than cutting it down. (Learning directly from this exhibit, as intended, I decided to leave an old hardwood standing in my own backyard. I have since witnessed three seasons of woodpecker offspring and have enjoyed eye contact with a screech owl who recently established residence.)

In terms of animal welfare, we must always be vigilant. If our critics correctly identify deficiencies in this area, we should move swiftly to remedy them. However, most good zoos are well ahead of their animal welfare critics and are able to anticipate and prevent animal welfare problems before they occur. It may be useful to ask whether zoo goals are consistent with general principles of animal welfare. This assumes that zoos already have a responsible animal welfare position from which to begin a dialogue, and I believe they do. Unfortunately, some animal welfare extremists are very difficult to dialogue with. We can only confront them with the record of our successes and with accurate, truthful information.

Zoo Atlanta experienced such an exchange when we introduced peregrine falcons to the city of Atlanta several years ago, as part of a program to restore this native bird in the area. Such programs had already been successfully undertaken in other cities. Working with the Georgia Department of Natural Resources and the Georgia Power Company, we placed young peregrines in training boxes atop the Georgia Power building in downtown Atlanta. Here they were fed, nurtured, and eventually released. We

A newborn Komodo dragon struggles to free itself from its egg case at the National Zoo in Washington, D.C. Zoo Atlanta now displays two of these creatures, the world's largest carnivorous lizard.
(Photograph by Jessie Cohen)

hoped they would return to this site after their first winter migration down the Atlantic flyway to South America. Naturally, we sought considerable publicity about our efforts, stressing our contributions to the larger effort to save this species from extinction. We were confident that our community would appreciate the program and rejoice as these rare birds matured, nested, and produced offspring. Soon after the story broke, however, we received an irate letter from a local citizen, who soon began a petition. She feared that our few peregrines, being birds of prey, would endanger the lives of local songbirds. She was misinformed in the matter, but we were unable to convince her of our good intentions. She assumed that a high density of peregrines would ensue from our release, but we knew that only a few pairs could possibly share our city's skyline, since these birds are fiercely territorial and protect large ranges for themselves. We reasoned that an occasional songbird might be taken, but that the peregrines were much more likely to feed on the numerous pigeons and starlings. It was a standoff. No meaningful dialogue could arise out of this argument. And now, several years later, our total population of peregrines is just three birds.

Zoo Atlanta staff have also cooperated with government officials to benefit bald eagles. In 1985 the zoo received its first pair of bald eagles from the U.S. Fish and Wildlife Service. The birds had been severely injured and subsequently rehabilitated, but they were not healthy enough to return to the wild. Each year hundreds of raptors (hawks, owls, and eagles) are injured by the thoughtless acts of people, usually through careless shooting. Incredible as it may seem, in the state of Georgia in 1992, two mature bald eagles were discovered shot to death, presumably on purpose.

Zoo Atlanta's injured eagles needed a large enclosure with a complex series of habitat features. At that time, we had no bird experts on our staff, so we sought assistance from Ron Morris, curator of birds at the North Carolina Zoo. Ron designed a habitat that our staff was able to build at very low cost. The environment contained a number of strong perching areas and a shallow, freshwater pond. We fed them a varied diet, appropriate for eagles, but once a week they received live rainbow trout, and it was quite fun to watch them interact with the fish.

Zoo professionals would prefer to provide "live food" for predatory animals, but the public expresses mixed feelings about predation in the zoo. However, our visitors apparently draw the line at fish, perhaps because of the widespread public enthusiasm for this universal sport. At Zoo Atlanta, we also feed live trout to our Indian gavials (a slender-snouted crocodile), and there is always a good crowd at feeding time. When we rebuild our sea lion facilities, we plan to extend the practice to them. It is a healthy procedure for many predatory animals, including bears, otters, and many cats. Properly explained to the public, and carefully planned, the consumption of live food is an important feature of the naturalistic zoo. Hediger may have addressed the problem best in his book *Man and Animal in the Zoo*: "The only principle on which the feeding of zoo animals should be based is that the food must be as natural as possible."

Recently, when federal facilities in Patuxent, Maryland, closed, we had the opportunity to obtain breeding pairs of bald eagles. Enthusiastic about the prospects of breeding the animals, we arranged to transport our birds to the nearby Chattahoochee Nature Center, which has developed an impressive educational program built around these birds. We negotiated on behalf of Che-Haw Park (a zoo in the south Georgia city of Albany) to send them one of the breeding pairs, and we took the other one. Che-Haw's birds laid eggs the first year, and by the second year they had actually released a young bird into the wild.

We at Zoo Atlanta are much closer to success as this book goes to press, but the circumstances are unusual. An egg was produced on March 11 amidst a flurry of copulations, with a second egg expected two days thereafter. However, Atlanta experienced an unusually severe snowstorm on March 12, and we must now await the effects of this environmental intrusion on the condition of the eggs. What timing! But that is the nature of the zoo business. If we are successful, we will work with the Georgia Department of Natural Resources to reintroduce the zoo-born eagles to the wild.

In spite of our considerable variability, zoos and aquariums do work toward useful goals, in the same way as museums, libraries, and universities. But we must also identify an agenda for the future of zoos, and we can do this best by acknowledging the errors of our past. Zoos in general have been slow to embrace conservation, slow to develop meaningful education programs, slow to cooperate with one another, slow to operate in a business-like manner, slow to hire highly qualified staff, and slow to broaden their outlook. All of these actions must take priority in the future. We work on these areas every day at Zoo Atlanta.

The first concept we adhere to is that zoos must enlighten the public and inspire action to save wildlife and the habitats in which they live. We must tell the story of wildlife conservation in such a way that will move people to participate. We cannot promote a "doomsday" curriculum, because people who lose hope will not participate. We should focus our story on solutions and on programs that are working. The zoo needs to be an inspiring place, a model of effective action. That is the main reason why naturalism in the zoo is so important. When you walk into the zoo, your spirits should be uplifted. I think this really happens at our zoo today. Only then can you learn and be moved to action. Indeed, psychologists have demonstrated that stimulating environments are more likely to be enjoyed and remembered.

Equally important, we must maintain our zoo animals in humane, naturalistic environments, in which their natural behavior patterns are enhanced by the quality of their surroundings and the people who care for them. Their physical and psychological well-being must be carefully addressed. If we fail to provide our animals with responsive, successful environments, we will deserve any criticism we receive. Today we know how to create optimal animal environments, and the findings of field biologists together with new technology have made it possible for us to create effective simulations of natural habitats. A few zoos have pioneered such techniques. For instance, the Basel Zoo in Switzerland has utilized principles derived from the work of Heini Hediger to create a naturalistic pathway framing exhibits that otherwise are very close to the public. The Arizona-Sonora Desert Museum (read "zoo") leads as well, especially in using the most advanced rock-and-tree landscape technology, and is the origin of the now-famed Larson Company, manufacturers of the world's best artificial rocks and trees. Merv Larson, founder of the firm and former director of the museum, is now in high demand for his naturalistic rockwork. In a recent article in *Smithsonian* magazine, Larson explained: "Rocks have soul. Most people figure rocks are inanimate, but they're moving. They're being eroded, built up. They won't last forever." There are now other companies who offer similar services to zoos, since this type of technology has become very useful in building naturalistic/realistic zoo habitats. Our exhibits at Zoo Atlanta are full of magnificent examples of this type of "rockwork."

The Arizona-Sonora Desert Museum is a trendsetter in other ways, too. It was one of the first zoos to specialize according to regional zoo geography and weather, re-creating the desert habitats that surround the facility. Hediger was a strong proponent of this kind of specialization. The Arizona-Sonora Museum has a fine array of desert creatures of all kinds. Especially notable is its collection of insects, as it was one of the first zoos to exhibit insects on a large scale. We can only expect more invention from Tucson, since its new director is David Hancocks, the scholarly former director of the Woodland Park Zoo in Seattle. An architect by training, and a key advocate for zoo naturalism, Hancocks may be the most innovative zoo director in the world today. If there is a new wave in zoo exhibitry to come, it will surely arise first in Tucson.

Another innovative zoo director is Dr. Michael Robinson of the National Zoo, who has written most convincingly about the "biopark" concept. His biopark combines the best features of aquariums, botanical gardens, arboretums, natural-history and culture museums, and zoos to create, as he put it, "a holistic form of bioexhibitry." The biopark interconnects those elements which have been disconnected by institutions with a narrow focus. In his own words:

> It is regrettable that we so arrange our public institutions that one can only see the skeleton of an elephant at a great distance from the place where one can see the live animal. We say, in effect, look at the elephant's skull and then catch the bus to the zoo and look at the elephant's head!

In the biopark, argues Robinson, we can learn about human history, art, and artifacts, but we should also learn about the effects of homo sapiens on planet earth. As Robinson points out, the relationship of the National Zoo within the Smithsonian family provides a unique opportunity for holistic development and interpretation. The physical proximity of New York's Central Park Zoo and the American Museum of Natural History represents another opportunity for collaboration, likewise Chicago's Field Museum and its neighbor the Shedd Aquarium. Regretfully, such holistic collaboration is the exception rather than the rule.

Amazonia, Robinson's first holistic exhibit at the National Zoo, is now open to the public. It spectacularly unites the world of plants and animals, terrestrial and aquatic, under one immense roof. In Amazonia, visitors can experience the extraordinary expertise of Smithsonian scientists as they tell the story of tropical biodiversity and the struggle to protect it from human intervention. There is beauty in this place, and food for thought.

In a next generation of bioparks, Robinson foresees another kind of exhibit, where the doors of animal perception are opened at last. In such a place, visitors can see the world as animals see it, detecting odors outside the boundaries of human olfaction, hearing sounds that no person ever heard before. Here the unique specializations of creatures very different from ourselves will come alive to us as never before.

Robinson also has argued convincingly for the use of computers and robotics to tell the story of evolving intelligence, including the elusive construct of "artificial intelligence." With recent advances in robotic technology, zoos, museums, and aquariums have promoted short-term exhibitions of dinosaurs, giant insects, and sea creatures. These exhibits have been a great success with the public, adding life to the museum and a bit more fantasy to the zoo or aquarium. The St. Louis Zoo produced a lifesize, robotic version of Charles Darwin, who lectures daily about his theory of natural selection to visitors of the high-tech Living World interpretive center. Zoo Atlanta's interactive conservation center, now in the advanced stages of design, will provide a permanent role for robotic versions of recently extinct forms such as the Great Auk, the Dodo Bird, and the giant Irish Elk.

The race to exhibit robotics has demonstrated just how similar zoos, museums, and botanical gardens have become. Many zoos have become such successful landscapes that they have added "Botanical Gardens" to their name. Cincinnati was the first of many to extend its reach into this domain. In Atlanta, our nearby Callaway Gardens resort built a state-of-the-art butterfly house, and it recently added a raptor show to its zoological repertoire. Zoo Atlanta has ventured into art by commissioning sculpture (pioneered by the Philadelphia Zoo) and offering Artists Safaris at the zoo. Atlanta's science and technology museum, Sci-Trek, exhibited sea creatures in 1991. In the summer of

1993, both Zoo Atlanta and the Fernbank Natural History Museum will offer robotic dinosaur exhibits. We all seek to be more interactive, which is what our customers want, too.

In spite of these similarities and developments, zoos are still unique in their ability to successfully manage, breed, and exhibit a diversity of living creatures. We may use museum techniques to interpret nature, but we will always be the experts who have a license to exhibit wild creatures. The zoo may evolve into a biopark, but its proper position will require more keepers than taxidermists, more zoologists than horticulturists. In a zoo, when plants and animals compete for living space, the animals must win. The plants provide the ambience, but the wildlife are the centerpiece of our universe.

But exhibits that look good are not always good enough. Sometimes naturalistic enclosures work no better than cages. The psychological needs of the animals must be provided for as well, and we have been very careful to attend to this at Zoo Atlanta. Animals should be exhibited in their appropriate social groupings and exhibited as solitary animals only if that is how they naturally live in the wild. Male orangutans, for example, are generally solitary in nature, so it is appropriate for them to be solitary in the zoo. However, for breeding purposes, they must occasionally be brought together with females, and they should also be housed within view of other orangutans so that they can engage in their species-typical vocalizations.

Zoos must also continue to cooperate with other institutions, in order to promote rational, global, collective management of captive animal populations. We must be prepared to put our self-interests aside in order to deal with the priorities of objective animal management. As an example, take our famed gorilla Willie B. He happens to be a founder gorilla—a representative of his species with genes from the wilds of Cameroon in West Africa. Since he has no offspring, he has also been identified as an animal with a breeding priority, so that his genes may be added to increase the genetic diversity of the captive population, to keep it self-sustaining. We're fortunate that the loan of gorillas from the Yerkes Primate Center has given us an opportunity to socialize him and breed him right here in our zoo. But if we had not had these new gorillas, and if AAZPA's Species Survival Plan committee for gorillas had requested that he be moved to another facility for breeding, I would gladly let him go. As important as Willie B. is to our zoo, our visitors, and our community, his breeding potential within the captive gorilla population is more important. I do believe that Atlantans would understand, too, and that they would support Willie's move if that were the best way for him to produce an heir. But we were lucky. We were able to have him become socialized and start breeding right in front of his own adoring public. Still, we must always be prepared to subordinate our local self-interest for the larger and greater good of the survival of the species.

The zoo agenda must also take into account that zoos today are cultural institutions, and that they can provide local leadership in many ways. In Atlanta, our zoo is regarded as equal in importance to our major museums such as the High Museum of Art, to our science and technology museum, known as Sci-Trek, and to our local botanical garden. But this is not the case everywhere. When Atlanta hosted the Democratic National Convention in 1988, our benefactors at Ford organized a party for the press covering the event. One of the reporters, who was from a large West Coast city, later wrote a column somewhat critical of us. "Atlanta is the kind of city that considers its zoo to be a cultural institution," he wrote. He was right. We do consider it to be a cultural institution. His comments indicated to me that his own city did not recognize the cultural significance of its zoo, and that will be a serious impediment to its future. In order to be effective, zoos have to be highly regarded in their communities, as highly as other cultural institutions, in order to gain the participation and support they need.

The zoo's biggest constituency is the family, but zoos really can serve every segment of the community. At Zoo Atlanta we are always pleased by how many young couples, without children, come to the zoo. Some people, like me, even regard the zoo as romantic, a proper locale for a date. The zoo is exactly where I had my first two dates with my wife, and I have met others who courted at the zoo. A stroll through a naturalistic zoo is like a walk in the woods, providing beauty, tranquility, and mystery. In the spring, the zoo is alive with the sights and sounds of courtship. This is the best time to visit with a date!

One of the most important developments in recent years has been the privatization of zoos and aquariums, and this will likely be the way of the future. Because Zoo Atlanta was one of the first zoos to go private, we have learned many things about the process. Indeed, representatives from numerous local governments and groups in other cities have visited us to learn more about how to privatize their own zoos. We have learned that the best governance concept is a public/private partnership. Zoos must be able to manage themselves in businesslike ways, but governments should continue to help, especially by allocating funds (through bond issues and other methods) for new (and expensive) naturalistic exhibitry. In Atlanta, we jump-started our turnaround with $16 million in revenue bonds from the city of Atlanta and Fulton County, raising additional funds from private sources. But we have spent $26 million so far, will soon commence a $25 million second phase, and will probably need a third phase of funding before the end of the century. Recently, officials of the Los Angeles Zoo announced plans to renovate their zoo for a total cost of $250 million. Naturalizing zoos is an expensive proposition and generally requires access to both public and private funds.

In order to compete for private funds, however, zoos must

typically remove themselves from government operation, as Atlanta did. Nonprofit private management structures are the best way to go, for this reason and for the most efficient operations possible. Zoos must compete against all other forms of leisure activities, such as movie theaters, amusement parks, and sports events and must be free to behave like their competitors, marketing their product in trendy, creative ways.

As this book goes to press, zoos in Detroit, Memphis, San Francisco, and Apple Valley, Minnesota, are flirting with privatization, aspiring to join those who have already made the leap (Atlanta, Baltimore, Fort Worth, Phoenix). Many others are watching with interest to see how well we do. I'm willing to bet that this trend will continue into the next century, and the nonprofit model will become a dominant form of zoo management. Zoos should prosper in cities friendly to business, where corporations and foundations are flourishing. For example, Cushman & Wakefield's national CEO survey ranked the following cities as the best places to do business in 1991: Atlanta; Seattle; Tampa; Dallas/Fort Worth; Portland, Oregon; Columbus, Ohio; Cincinnati; Houston; Phoenix; and Indianapolis. Most of these cities have zoos that are very good right now. I expect each of them to prosper in the next few years.

Finally, the zoo agenda must take into account the growing importance of science and technology. Zoos will need to be solidly scientific in their approach, as we have tried so hard to be in Atlanta. They need to affiliate with universities and to attract talent from them. Scientists are being recruited by zoos more and more, and I believe that their presence will produce some very dramatic changes in the future.

Yes, not only Zoo Atlanta but the zoo world in general has certainly been involved in a revolution during the last twenty-five years—in exhibitry, in business operation, in science, and, most of all, in philosophy, outlook, and mission. This revolution has seen a lot of progress. But it is far from over. We still have a long way to go, but we are on the right path. Given the revolutionary trends, I expect zoos and aquariums to be dramatically transformed by the year 2000. At the turn of the century, the following descriptors should be quite accurate for both Zoo Atlanta and zoos and aquariums collectively:

- Zoos and aquariums will be recognized as the most effective type of conservation education organization in the world. There will be no institutions who do this job better. Zoo Atlanta, for example, has already won awards and grants for such programs.

- Zoos and aquariums will be routinely affiliated with research and teaching universities. Universities will come to regard zoos as a kind of laboratory for the study of animals, people, and landscapes. Other scholarly people will use the zoo as well. Management and business personnel, for example, will find opportunity in the zoo.

- Poets, artists, musicians, and writers will find inspiration at the zoo, and will produce works of art based on their experiences. Some of these works of art will be produced and performed in the zoo itself. We've already started this process at Zoo Atlanta, with our first artist-in-residence.

- Zoos and aquariums will be highly valued for expert consultation by national park systems of developing countries. Zoos will expand their current support of wildlife programs in connection with people in these countries, such as Zoo Atlanta's work in Rwanda's Akagera Park.

- Zoos and aquariums increasingly will be the last

refuge for endangered species. We will save many species by successfully propagating them in captivity, and our ark will be greatly enlarged in order to meet the demand.

- Zoos and aquariums will be leaders in the marketing of a conservation ethic, and leaders in environmental problem-solving worldwide. By working together with the best minds in our communities and addressing our huge, broad-based constituency, we will market conservation like it's never been marketed before. We will also work to bring other wildlife conservation organizations together, so that we may affect genuine, lasting change in the way we live on this fragile planet.

- Zoos and aquariums will provide the crucial link between local communities and global problems. Corporations that are becoming more environmentally conscious will help us in this regard, as will close relationships with foreign zoos and with wildlife conservationists in many countries.

For many years, a small cadre of zoo experts has been developing a position statement on conservation. Known as the World Zoo Conservation Strategy, it is linked to documents previously published by the IUCN/World Conservation Union. What is most wonderful about IUCN (International Union for the Conservation of Nature) is its leadership base; it is run almost entirely by volunteers. In fact, it is more of a network than an organization. A less attractive element is its dues structure. For a zoo to become a member, it must pay annual dues of $10,000! No wonder there are so few affiliated members from the zoo world.

IUCN published its *World Zoo Conservation Strategy* in 1980. Its goal was to "persuade the nations of the world to adopt ecologically sound development practices."

Furthermore, the document attempted to demonstrate that conservation contributes to the well-being of people as well as wildlife. Two additional documents were published in the 1990s: *Caring for the Earth* (1991) and *Global Biodiversity Strategy* (1992). Both booklets advocate a role in global conservation for the world's zoos and aquariums. For example, Actions 69 and 71 of the *Global Biodiversity Strategy* would, respectively, "strengthen the conservation role of zoological parks," and "strengthen collaboration among off-site and on-site conservation institutions, partly to enlarge the role of off-site facilities in species reintroduction, habitat restoration, and habitat rehabilitation." The written strategy of the world's zoos has now reached the advanced draft stage and will soon be available in final form. Its main conclusions have been made available for comment and discussion to members of the International Union of Directors of Zoological Gardens. Since this important document is nearing its final form, I will summarize, paraphrase, and integrate a few salient points herein:

- It is the task of zoos to heighten public and political awareness about the interdependence of life. Their collections of living animals should be used to optimize the telling of the whole conservation story.

- Zoos can contribute to conservation by shifting the use of available animal space from more common species toward more space for endangered species in coordinated, managed programs.

- Advanced reproductive technology must be utilized to preserve genetic material, and for the production of highly endangered species. Scientific resources should be nurtured to provide for these contributions to conservation. Zoos and their scientific partners are valuable sources of knowledge.
- Translocating zoo-bred stock back into wild habi-

tats is a logical, although challenging, outcome of support for wild populations.

■ To enlarge the vision of conservation, the *World Zoo Conservation Strategy* suggests that zoos and aquariums express their conservation commitments in their mission statements.

Scientists have recently estimated that more than 4,000 species of plants and animals are disappearing each year. The rate of extinction is especially rapid within the rain forests, where the world's greatest array of bio-diversity is located. The clearing of rain forests for timber, cattle farming, mining, and subsistence agriculture has been catastrophic—to the animals and plants and to the land itself. In the state of Georgia alone, more than 600 plants and animals are already on the endangered species list, including the right whale, the manatee, the bald eagle, and the indigo snake. Zoos have a big job to save wildlife and wild places. It is the fundamental reason for the existence of our zoo. Who would have thought that the infamous, dilapidated Atlanta zoo of 1984 could ever hope to address a challenge as big and important as this? But after all, that's the whole point of a revolution, isn't it?

TEN-YEAR CHRONOLOGY OF ATLANTA'S ZOO

1984	*Parade* magazine names the Atlanta Zoo as one of the ten worst zoos in America.
	The Atlanta Zoo is denied membership in the American Association of Zoological Parks & Aquariums (AAZPA).
	Dr. Terry L. Maple, a Georgia Tech professor of psychology, is named zoo director.
	A blue-ribbon citizen's committee develops a model for privatizing zoo management and for funding a new zoo.
1985	A new veterinary clinic opens, built with city funds.
	A nonprofit board assumes control of the zoo on December 5. Zoo Atlanta is born.
1986	The Atlanta Fulton County Recreation Authority issues $16 million in revenue bonds for the zoo. Zoo construction begins.
	The state-of-the-art zoo commissary is completed.
	The zoo and WSB air their first wildlife television special, with TV personality Virginia Gunn.
	A baby African elephant, Starlet O'Hara, arrives at the zoo. *USA Today* names her as one of America's most popular zoo animals.
	Bob Strickland, CEO of Trust Company Bank, agrees to chair the first capitol campaign. Atlanta corporations donate more than $4 million to the zoo.
1987	Flamingo Plaza, the first new animal exhibit, opens.
	The Metropolitan Foundation honors Zoo Atlanta for excellence in nonprofit management.
	Zoo Atlanta is honored for its role in the WATL Emmy award for a zoo television special.
	Zoo Atlanta is accredited by AAZPA.
1988	The Ford African Rainforest opens, the orangutan exhibit opens, and Yerkes gorillas and orangutans arrive.

	The Metropolitan Foundation again honors Zoo Atlanta as Best Managed Nonprofit Corporation in the city.
	"Search for the Red Ape," the zoo television special with WSB, dominates its time slot. The show wins a ratings contest against "ALF" and wins a second Emmy.
1989	The zoo celebrates its hundredth birthday and announces its theme: "Conservation Leadership for Our Second Century."
	The Ford African Rainforest exhibit wins the AAZPA Significant Achievement Award.
	The zoo opens its Masai Mara exhibit for a giraffe, a zebra, an antelope, an ostrich, a crowned crane, and other plains species.
	Zoo attendance hits an all-time high of 798,000 visitors. Friends of the Zoo memberships hit 50,000.
	The first gorillas are born at the zoo. Willie B. starts to breed.
	Zoo Atlanta hosts the most successful and best attended Southern regional meeting in the history of AAZPA.
	Peregrine falcon chicks are released atop the Georgia Power building downtown.
1990	The WSB special "Wild, Alive, Endangered" wins a third Emmy award.
	The zoo opens three exhibits: Sumatran Tiger Forest, Black Rhino, and Monkeys of Makokou.
	The zoo wins its second consecutive Significant Achievement Award from AAZPA for the Masai Mara exhibit.
	The zoo is awarded the opportunity to host the 1994 national conference of AAZPA.
	Rare aldabra tortoises hatch at the zoo.
	Zoo Atlanta is named one of the top ten zoos in the country by *City/State Magazine*.

1991	The zoo successfully stages the "Days of the Living Dinosaurs" exhibit, achieving a record for fall attendance.
	A peregrine falcon released in 1989 returns to Atlanta with a mate.
	The Georgia Wildlife Federation honors Zoo Atlanta as Conservation Organization of the Year.
	The zoo acquires its second black rhino from San Francisco.
	Michael Warikhe, "the rhino man," visits Zoo Atlanta.
	The zoo receives a year-end gift of $1.5 million from an anonymous foundation.
1992	Koalas from the San Diego Zoo are exhibited in Atlanta for three months. The zoo stages a "Giant Insects" traveling exhibit in the fall.
	Zoo Atlanta hosts the Elephant Management Workshop.
	Zoo Atlanta is reaccredited by AAZPA.
	The new zoo administrative building opens. Friends of Zoo Atlanta and Zoo Atlanta staff are housed in one location.
	A Sumatran tiger cub is born at the zoo.
	The peregrine falcons return. A female lays three eggs atop the Marriott Marquis downtown.
1993	The zoo hosts the annual convention of the American Association of Zoo Keepers.
	Komodo dragons are acquired on loan from the National Zoo.
	Zoo Atlanta and its "Friends" support group are merged into one nonprofit organization.
1994	Zoo Atlanta will host the annual convention of AAZPA.

EPILOGUE

MUSINGS OF A SILVERBACK

The only meeting place that the civilized world has negotiated between the absence and presence of the wild is the zoo.
Charles Siebert

In the summer of 1984, I dared to hope that someday our zoo would be portrayed as a model for other zoos. At that time, our zoo was so imperfect, so flawed, and so far out of touch with the mainstream that it required a complete overhaul of the operating system. And yet, other zoos had an equal or greater need for change. What would it take to change all zoos? Maybe, I dared to consider, it would take a real phoenix story, rags to riches, the proverbial silk purse. In many ways, we are that model.

One effect of the Atlanta Zoo story is raised standards. I have seen dramatic changes in communities no longer inclined to look the other way when their zoo begins to drift. Zoo people are more vigilant today, recognizing that mediocrity can quickly turn into complete failure. One licensing agency, the USDA, enforces its toughened standards like never before. For its part, the AAZPA accreditation committee is determined to act sooner when a zoo gets into trouble. The Atlanta Zoo story taught us this much: Mismanagement in a single institution undermines confidence in the entire zoo profession. The zoo industry is doing a much better job of elevating its standards, monitoring compliance, and policing the membership. These are comforting developments for zoos and aquariums, and I am personally gratified that the clean-up of Zoo Atlanta played a role in the betterment of all zoos.

Wherever I go to talk about the zoo, a grateful public tries to give me all of the credit for turning the zoo around. I don't deserve such accolades, since nothing could be further from the truth. Zoo Atlanta has been a team effort, a community effort. It has been a job well done over a period of years by a network of corporate and community leaders, more than 100 zoo staff people, hundreds of dedicated volunteers, and thousands of supporters. The animals themselves played an important role, too. It was, after all, their story.

Every city with a zoo has a "zoo man" (or woman) who is the focal point of the endeavor, but success depends on the hard work and commitment of the many who believe in the zoo dream. Zoos "turn around" when a community is ready and able to do the job. They turn when the constituency supporting the cause is powerful enough to make the point. They turn when the zoo has priority. Atlanta in 1984 was ready and able to revitalize its zoo. Adrift in a sea of priorities, the zoo was finally singled out for a life preserver. We zoo directors get to pilot the ark, but it is surely propelled by the focused energy of its community. I am happy that I could play a role in this wonderful phoenix story.

Zoo Atlanta has twice been accredited since 1984, evoking numerous compliments, and it has twice been recognized by AAZPA for significant achievements in exhibit design. The zoo has been honored as the best-managed nonprofit corporation in Atlanta, and its local television programs have won five Emmy awards. Zoo staff have received prestigious grants from the Institute for Museum Services, the National Science Foundation, the National Geographic Society, the National Endowment for the Arts, and the New York Zoological Society's Nixon-Griffis Fund.

In 1990 the zoo was selected by the Georgia Wildlife Federation as its Conservation Organization of the Year, while *City/State Magazine* named the zoo as one of America's ten best in 1989. Its phenomenal attendance and membership growth is an industry legend. Willie B. now graces the cover of AAZPA's membership directory "Zoological Parks and Aquariums in the Americas," testimony to the incredible story of our full acceptance into the world community of competent zoos. In 1994 Zoo Atlanta will host AAZPA's annual convention. Zoo Atlanta has come a long, long way in a few, short years.

My zoo life has required every skill and attribute that my primate origins foretold. My leadership, patience, flexibility, optimism, tenacity, confidence, toughness, commitment, and wisdom have all been tapped, tested, and stretched in this job. As this book is published, I enter my tenth year at the helm. It has been a wild and woolly ride.

For each of these ten years, my staff and I have operated inside the zoo revolution. We are still zealous in our pursuit of excellence, and in this way I hope that the zoo continues to reinvent itself. Because we are a scientific zoo, we recognize opportunity, and we resist inertia. We want to stay young, experimental, and lean. We can't imagine ourselves growing old, theoretical, and obese. And so we must constantly renew and revisit our mission. What does it mean to be a zoo revolutionary? It means long workdays, new ideas, and self-criticism. If zoos were more self-critical, we wouldn't be such easy targets for outside criticism. A moving zoo is not an easy target.

If we at Zoo Atlanta are comfortable with change, it is because we changed so fast. Change has been good to us. We are comfortable with change, too, because all good businesses must change or die. Our business mentors taught us well. As a business we seek to be successful by business criteria. The financially strong zoo or aquarium builds reserves for the tough times, endowments to continue its most worthy endeavors, and profits that spin off to its stockholders, the wildlife, and wildlife habitats. The urgency of conservation requires financially fit zoos.

Often, I am asked to give advice to others who are engaged in a "turn-around" crisis. Of course, no two situations are exactly alike, so this is tough to do. Much of what we accomplished in Atlanta was just plain common sense. For what it's worth, here are five things worth doing in a crisis:

1. Admit your mistakes, tell the whole truth, and ask for help from anyone who is willing to provide it.
2. Get out of your office and talk to the community. Articulate a vision and promote your dream to anyone who will listen.
3. Surround yourself with the best people you can find. Recruit from the best zoos and companies for staff and board. Challenge your staff with a big job, get out of the way while they do it, and hold them accountable.
4. Solve the really tough problems first. Demonstrate your confidence in the future by taking risks.
5. Aim high; think big; demand excellence; expect to win.

Intuitively, this was how I approached our crisis. I hadn't learned these things in a textbook. They were simply reasonable responses to a challenging situation. The crisis was so deep that there were no impediments to thinking big. The situation seemed so impossible that no one bothered to advise me that I shouldn't think this way or demand excellence so quickly. In order to begin, I had to increase my resource base so that I could recruit winning staff, and I had to find creative solutions to overcome bureaucratic barriers. Fortunately, there were some big thinkers in government and industry who believed in the zoo. The public spoke loud and the mandate was clear. In the business community, the magic of our corporate leaders made it all work.

On my first day at work, I came to the conclusion that the entire zoo would have to change. And that is exactly what we did. In nine years we invented Zoo Atlanta, and Zoo Atlanta continues to reinvent itself now. It is an institution dedicated to flexibility and change.

The community dreamed of a zoo to match the greatness of its people. In many ways the zoo *is* truly great, but it is not so good that it won't get better. As long as the community pays attention, Zoo Atlanta will continue to improve.

Looking into my crystal ball, I see a promising future for this zoo and for all zoos and aquariums. Zoos will be more popular than ever, and with their increased focus on science and education, they will be key partners in the movement to improve science education in America. In conservation, zoos and aquariums will share in the credit when we save this planet: We are part of the solution in this new epoch of change and public service. We will be lightning rods for community awareness, a locus for conservation action, and a powerful resource for environmental problem solving. Our children will see in their zoo a reflection of the good, green earth that surrounds them.

Several years ago, when I was on a one-hour television interview show, the host opened up with the question "How can this zoo hope to be great when it is so small?" After an hour of give and take, and an exhaustive review of our accomplishments, programs, and activities, the interviewer concluded: "I had no idea that the zoo was so big!" Zoo Atlanta is not big; but it does big things.

In a very real sense, Willie B., Starlet the elephant, and Boma the rhino have sounded their public appeal. Saving the world's wildlife is an awesome challenge. They deserve our best effort.

BIBLIOGRAPHY

Akeley, C. E. 1923. *In brightest Africa*. New York: Garden City.

Aspinall, John. 1986. The Howletts Gorilla bands. In *Primates: The Road to self-sustaining populations*, ed. K. Benirschke, 465–70. New York: Springer-Verlag.

Beck, B. B., and M. L. Power. 1989. Correlates of sexual and maternal competence in captive gorillas. *Zoo Biology* 7 (no. 4): 339–50.

Benchley, B. 1940. *My life in a man-made jungle*. Boston: Little, Brown.

Benirschke, K. 1975. Biomedical research. In *Research in zoos and aquariums*. Washington, D.C.: National Academy of Sciences.

———. 1986. Primates: *The Road to self-sustaining populations*. New York: Springer-Verlag, Inc.

Bennis, W., and B. Nanus. 1985. *Leaders*. New York: Harper & Row.

Chiszar, D., J. B. Murphy, and W. Iliff. 1990. For zoos. *Psychological Record* 40:3–13.

Conway, W. G. 1969. Zoos: Their changing roles. *Science* 161:48–52.

Davenport, R. K. 1967. The orang-utan in Sabah. *Folia Primatologica* 5:247–63.

De Boer, L. The World Zoo Conservation Strategy. Unpublished manuscript. Amsterdam: National Foundation for Research in Zoological Gardens.

De Waal, F. B. M. 1982. *Chimpanzee politics*. London: Jonathan Cape.

———. 1989. *Peacemaking among primates*. Cambridge: Harvard University Press.

Erwin, J., T. Maple, and G. Mitchell, eds. 1979. *Captivity and behavior*. New York: Van Nostrand Reinhold.

Garner, R. L. 1896. *Gorillas and chimpanzees*. London: Osgood McIlvaine & Co.

Graham, E. C., and R. Roberts. 1992. *The Real ones: Four generations of the first family of Coca-Cola*. Fort Lee, N.J.: Barricade Books.

Gruber, H. E. 1974. *Darwin on man*. New York: E. P. Dutton & Co.

Hancocks, D. 1983. Gorillas go natural. *Animal Kingdom* 86 (no. 3): 10–16.

Hartley, M., and A. Commire. 1991. *Breaking the silence*. New York:

Signet/Penguin Books.
Hediger, H. 1964. *Wild Animals in Captivity*. New York: Dover Publications.
———. 1969. *Man and animal in the zoo*. London: Routledge & Kegan Paul.
———. 1982. Sex and age differences in the avoidance of reptile exhibits by zoo visitors. *Zoo Biology* 1 (no. 3): 263–70.
Hunt, H., and Ogden, J. J. 1991. Selected aspects of the nesting ecology of American alligators in the Okefenokee Swamp. *J. Herpetology* 28 (no. 4): 448–53.
Jamieson, D. 1985. Against zoos. In *In defense of animals*, ed. P. Singer, 109–17. Oxford: Basil Blackwell.
Konner, M. 1982. *The Tangled wing*. New York: Holt, Rinehart, & Winston.
Kotler, P., and E. L. Roberto. 1989. *Social marketing*. New York: The Free Press.
Lorenz, K. *King Solomon's ring*. 1952. New York: Thomas Y. Crowell.
———. 1966. *On aggression*. New York: Harcourt, Brace, & World.
Maple, T. L. 1979. Primate psychology in historical perspective. In *Captivity and behavior*, eds. J. Erwin, T. L. Maple, and G. Mitchell. New York: Van Nostrand Reinhold Co.
———. 1980. *Orangutan behavior*. New York: Van Nostrand Reinhold Co.
———. 1982. Toward a unified zoo biology. *Zoo Biology* 1 (no. 1): 1–4.
Maple, T. L., and M. P. Hoff. 1982. *Gorilla behavior*. New York: Van Nostrand Reinhold Co.
Maple, T. L., and D. W. Matheson. 1973. *Aggression, hostility and violence*. New York: Holt, Rinehart & Winston.
Maple, T. L., and A. Warren-Leubecker. 1983. Variability in the parental conduct of captive great apes and some generalizations to humankind. In *Child abuse: The Nonhuman primate data*, eds. M. Reite and N. G. Caine. New York: Alan R. Liss, Inc.
Maple, T. L., E. L. Zucker, and M. B. Dennon. 1979. Cyclic proceptivity in a captive female orang-utan. *Behavioural Processes* 4:53–59.
Marcellini, D., and T. A. Janssen. 1988. Visitor behavior in the National Zoo's reptile house. *Zoo Biology* 7:329–38.
Markowitz, H. 1982. *Behavioral enrichment in the zoo*. New York: Van

Nostrand Reinhold Co.

Montgomery, S. 1991. *Walking with the great apes*. Boston: Houghton Mifflin.

Morris, D. 1980. *Animal days*. New York: William Morrow & Co.

Ogden, J. J., T. W. Finlay, and T. L. Maple. 1990. Gorilla adaptations to naturalistic environments. *Zoo Biology* 9 (no. 2): 107–21.

Perkins, L. A. 1989. An examination of the influences of the captive environment on activity in orangutans. Master's thesis, Georgia Institute of Technology, Atlanta.

Peters, T. 1987. *Thriving on chaos*. New York: Harper & Row.

Petersen, D. E., and J. Hillkirk. 1991. *A Better idea*. Boston: Houghton Mifflin Co.

Rachels, J. 1976. Do animals have a right to liberty? In *Animal rights and human obligations*, eds. T. Regan and P. Singer. Englewood Cliffs, N.J.: Prentice-Hall.

Reis, B. 1987. Happy hippos, cheerful chimps. *Smithsonian Magazines* 17 (no. 11): 107–14.

Robinson, M. H. 1990. The Once and future zoo. *Smithsonian Magazine* 20:198–205.

Rutherford, F. J., and A. Ahlgren. 1989. *Science for all Americans*. New York: Oxford University Press.

Siebert, C. 1991. Where have all the animals gone? The Lamentable extinction of zoos. *Harper's* (May): 49–58.

Sommer, R. 1973. What do we learn at the zoo? *Natural History* 81 (no. 7): 26–27, 84–85.

———. 1974. *Tight spaces*. Englewood Cliffs, N.J.: Prentice-Hall.

Stevens, E. F. 1991. Flamingo breeding: The Role of group displays. *Zoo Biology* 10 (no. 1): 53–64.

Watson, J. B. 1928. *Psychological care of the infant and child*. New York: Norton.

Wegeforth, H. M., and N. Morgan. 1953. *It began with a roar*. San Diego: Zoological Society of San Diego.

Wineman, J., and Y. K. Choi. 1991. Spatial/visual properties of zoo exhibition. *Curator* 34 (no. 4): 304–15.

Yerkes, R. M. 1925. *Almost human*. New York: Century.

INDEX

Page numbers in italic refer to illustrations.